The Vegetarian
Treasure Chest

The Vegetarian Treasure Chest

Winifred Graham

Published by Quicksilver Productions
P. O. Box 340, Ashland, Oregon 97520 USA

Library of Congress Cataloging in Publication Data

Graham, Winifred, 1896–
    Vegetarian Treasure Chest

    Includes index.
    1. Vegetarian cookery. I. Title.
TX837.G673   1983   641.5;636   82–62710
ISBN 0-930356-33-0

Originally published in the United Kingdom by
Thorsons Publishers Limited
Copyright© Winifred Graham 1980

Cover illustration by Conni Morton
cover concept by Lorena Laforest Bass
Cover art © 1983 Quicksilver Productions

First published in the United States 1983

1 2 3 4 5 6 7 8 9   90 89 88 87 86 85 84 83

INTERNATIONAL STANDARD BOOK NUMBER: 0-930356-33-0
LIBRARY OF CONGRESS CATALOG CARD NUMBER: 82-062710

Published by Quicksilver Productions, Ashland, Oregon 97520

Table of Contents

Chapter One — Soups

Chapter One — Soups

Stocks

1 pound vegetables (your choice)
4 cups water

Vegetable stocks may be made from practically any vegetable. However, be aware that onions and chicory have a strong flavor, potatoes make a cloudy stock, and beets color the stock vividly.

Wash, but do not peel, all the vegetables. In a large, covered saucepan bring the water to a boil and add vegetables, including all outside leaves. Bring to second boil; then reduce heat and simmer from 1-2 hours.

Clear Vegetable Broth

4 cups stock
1 tablespoon butter or margarine
1 teaspoon Miso or Tamari Soy Sauce
1 small bay leaf
Salt to taste
A few sprigs of parsley

Simmer all the ingredients together, except the parsley, for 20–30 minutes in a covered saucepan. Add finely chopped parsley just before serving.

Unless otherwise stated, quantities are given for 6 servings.

Scotch Broth

¼ cup pearl barley
5 cups stock
2 large carrots
1 rutabaga
2 leeks
3 large onions
3 large potatoes
6 tablespoons margarine or oil
6 teaspoons Miso or Tamari Soy Sauce
Sea salt
1 tablespoon cream

Bring 2 cups of the stock to a boil in a covered saucepan over high heat, add the barley, reduce the heat to low, and simmer 1½ hours until tender. Peel and cut the vegetables into bite-size pieces, then sauté for 8–10 minutes in a saucepan with the melted margarine. Add 3 cups of stock and simmer until the vegetables are tender. Mix all the ingredients together, except the cream, and simmer for 10–15 minutes. Stir in the cream and serve. This soup is a meal in itself.

Puréed Beet Soup

8 small beets
1 shallot, chopped (omit if using fruit juice)
1½ cups clear vegetable stock or
   Strained orange, grape or grapefruit juice
Pinch ground cloves
Salt and cayenne pepper
1 tablespoon honey
Juice of 1 lemon
Garnish of sour cream

Scrub, then add the beets and shallot to 2 cups of boiling water in a covered saucepan. Reduce the heat and simmer for 20 minutes. Strain and keep the liquid. Skin and cut the beets into small pieces; then purée with the shallot in a blender, adding some of the beet water or stock if the purée becomes too thick to blend. Stir in the seasonings, honey, and lemon juice; and thin with stock and beet liquid, but do not make it too thin. Chill well and serve garnished with sour cream.

Variation: For a tasty variation of this recipe, leave out the shallot and replace the vegetable stock with grape, orange, or grapefruit juice as soup stock.

Thin Borscht

3 medium beets, raw
3 carrots
3 shallots
½ small cabbage (optional)
2 leeks
4 tablespoons oil
5 cups vegetable stock
1 large bay leaf
2 tablespoons lemon juice
Salt to taste
1 teaspoon honey
Garnish of sour cream

Clean, peel, and cut all the vegetables, except one beet, into small pieces. Heat the oil in a thick saucepan, add the vegetables, and sauté over medium heat for 3 minutes. Stir well and cook over low heat for 8 more minutes. Pour in the stock, cover, and simmer gently until the vegetables are tender. Add the bay leaf, lemon juice, salt, and honey and continue to simmer for 5 more minutes. Strain through a sieve or colander. Grate the remaining beet into the soup. Serve, hot or cold, with a heaping tablespoon of sour cream on top of each serving.

Cherry and Beet Soup

18 small beets
1 tablespoon onion, finely minced
1 medium (16-ounce) can of Bing
   sweet cherries, pitted
3 cloves
1 cup boiling water
1½ tablespoons honey
Salt
Juice of 1 lemon or lime
Garnish of sour cream

Scrub the beets and either grate or thinly slice them. Add the onion and beets to 5 cups of boiling water in a covered saucepan; reduce the heat and simmer for 25 minutes. Then strain, but do not press, the beets; save the water and discard the beet pulp. Add the cherries and cloves to 1 cup of boiling water in a small saucepan, reduce the heat immediately and simmer for 10 minutes. Add the honey, salt, and lemon or lime juice to the beet juice liquid; then mix the cherries and their liquid with the beet juice. Chill well, and serve each helping topped with sour cream.

Fresh Asparagus Cream Soup

1 pound fresh asparagus
2 cups water
2 cups milk
4 tablespoons butter
5 tablespoons flour
Salt, pepper and dash of nutmeg
Garnish of parsley or chervil

Wash and cut the asparagus into 1-inch lengths. Set the tender tips to one side. Simmer the rest of the stalks for 30 minutes in a covered pan with 2 cups of water. Strain, keep the water and discard the stalks. Simmer the tips in the same water for 5-10 minutes, strain, and keep the tips and water in separate bowls. Add the milk to the asparagus water, set aside.

Sauce:
Melt the butter in the top of a double boiler, stir in the flour until blended, and cook for 3 minutes or until it bubbles. Slowly add the milk and asparagus water, stirring in a little at a time, and simmer for 5 minutes. Add the asparagus tips and season. Serve hot, garnished with chopped parsley or chervil. Makes 4-6 servings.

Cream of Celery Soup

1 large head of celery
1 small onion
4 tablespoons butter
4 cups stock with plenty of celery water in it
5 tablespoons flour
1 teaspoon Miso or Tamari Soy Sauce
1 teaspoon celery salt
Chopped celery leaves

Wash and cut the celery into ½-inch strips. Peel and cube the onion. Melt 1 tablespoon of butter in a saucepan, add the celery, and sauté over medium–low heat for 5 minutes, stirring often. This helps to bring out the flavor. Add 1 cup of boiling stock or water and simmer until tender.

Melt the rest of the butter in a saucepan, and sauté the onion until golden. Stir in the flour and cook over low heat for 5 minutes. Add the remaining 3 cups of stock, bring to a low boil, and cook until thickened. Add the celery and stock, lower the heat, and simmer for 15–20 minutes. Add the Miso, celery salt, and chopped celery leaves. Simmer for 5 more minutes, then serve.

Variation: To make this a richer soup, use cream or milk as part of the stock instead of water. Be sure not to boil it, however! Heat to just below the boiling point. To make a creamy soup, purée the celery in a blender after cooking.

Cream of Broccoli Soup

2 teaspoons onion, minced
½ green pepper, chopped
2 tablespoons butter or margarine
1½ cups (¾ pound fresh) broccoli
Dash of milk
½ cup sour cream
½ teaspoon curry powder
Salt and cayenne pepper
Chopped chives for garnish

Wash, chop, and cook the broccoli in a covered saucepan with ½ cup of boiling water, reduce the heat and simmer until tender. Drain and finely chop. Sauté the onion and green pepper in a frying pan with the melted butter. When soft, purée in a blender with the cooked broccoli. If the purée becomes too thick to blend, add a little water. Then blend in a dash of milk and the sour cream. Mix in the curry powder and season to taste with salt and cayenne pepper. Add more milk and blend to a creamy consistency. Garnish with chives or sour cream.

This soup has a delicate flavor and may be served hot or cold. If serving hot, heat over medium temperature to just below the boiling point. Do not boil this soup—it will ruin the flavor.

Cream of Corn Soup

4–6 ears of sweet corn or
*   2–3 cups canned sweet corn kernels*
Warm milk
¼ cup onion, diced
¼ cup green pepper, diced
Butter or margarine
½ teaspoon turmeric
Salt and cayenne pepper
Fresh dill or basil
1 cup Half and Half
Garnish of parsley, chives or green onions

Cook the corn in water then score the centers of the kernels with a fork to release the milk. Cut the corn from the cobs and scrape the ears carefully over a bowl so that nothing is lost (or use 2–3 cups canned, drained corn kernels). Purée the corn in a blender with a dash of warm milk. After blending, strain the corn to remove the little sharp skins.

Sauté the onions and green pepper in a frying pan with melted butter; then purée in the blender. Add a dash of milk if the purée becomes too thick to blend. Add the turmeric, salt, and cayenne pepper; and blend both purées together. Cut a sprig of fresh dill with sharp scissors (approximately 1 teaspoonful), or use 1 level teaspoon of basil, and add to the purée. Thin this thick purée with 1 cup or less of Half and Half to desired consistency. Garnish with chopped chives, parsley, or green onions. The turmeric gives this soup a lovely golden color.

Cream of Spinach Soup

1½ pounds (2 bunches) spinach
2 tablespoons vegetable oil
1 onion, chopped
1 teaspoon honey
Salt and pepper
1 teaspoon dried tarragon
½ cup Half and Half
Chopped parsley for garnish

Rinse the spinach twice, using first a warm water rinse and then a cold water rinse. Heat the oil in a large saucepan, add the chopped onion, and sauté gently for 3 minutes. Add the spinach, honey, seasonings, and tarragon. (Do not add water; simply use the water that is on the spinach leaves from washing them.) Cover tightly and steam over very low heat for 5 to 10 minutes until tender. Purée in a blender, adding enough Half and Half to make a consistency as thick as cream. Garnish with parsley. The flavor of this soup is improved if it is left to stand for a few hours before it is served, either hot or cold. If serving hot, be sure to heat to just below the boiling point. Do not boil as boiling spoils the flavor of cream soups.

Cream of Tomato Soup

½ cup onions, diced
½ cup carrots, chopped
3 tablespoons butter or margarine
5 cups tomatoes, skinned and chopped
Salt and pepper
2 teaspoons honey
6 teaspoons lemon juice
1½ tablespoons arrowroot or cornstarch
1 cup cream

Melt the butter in a deep saucepan, and sauté the onions and carrots for 3 minutes, then add the skinned tomatoes, salt, and pepper. (The easiest way to skin tomatoes is to drop them into boiling water for 3 minutes, drain and peel.) Simmer for 15 minutes, then purée the mixture in the blender. Pour back into the saucepan, add the honey and lemon juice, and simmer gently for 5 minutes. Blend the arrowroot and cream together in a bowl, add to the soup, and stir constantly with a whisk until blended. Continue to simmer until soup has thickened in consistency.

Serve hot or cold.

Lettuce Soup with Almonds

1 medium iceburg lettuce
1 small romaine lettuce
6 green onions, minced
2 tablespoons butter or oil
1 teaspoon turmeric
Salt and pepper
⅓ cup water
1 cup milk
1 cup Half and Half
1 cup vegetable stock
Garnish of ½ cup toasted almonds

Wash and finely shred the lettuce. Melt the butter in a saucepan and sauté the onions for 2 minutes. Add the lettuce, seasonings, and ⅓ cup water; cover and simmer until tender. Set aside 2 tablespoons of this mixture and purée the rest in the blender. Gently stir into the 2 tablespoons you set aside: the milk, Half and Half, and vegetable stock. Blend with the purée and serve hot or icy cold, garnished with toasted almonds. If serving hot, be sure to heat the milk, Half and Half, and stock before adding to the purée.

Mushroom Soup

½ pound mushrooms
3 tablespoons butter or oil
1 small onion
½ stalk of celery
¼ pound green beans
4 cups stock
1 teaspoon Miso or Tamari Soy Sauce
Salt
Parsley or chives

Wash, but do not peel, the mushrooms; cut them into thin slices. Melt the butter in a frying pan and sauté the mushrooms for 2 minutes. Clean the rest of the vegetables, cut into thin slices, and steam in a covered saucepan with a small amount of salted water until tender. Put the stock into a saucepan, add the cooked vegetables, except the mushrooms, bring to a boil, then reduce the heat and simmer for 30 minutes. Add the mushrooms, and Miso, salt to taste, and simmer for 5 more minutes. Serve with chopped chives or parsley on top.

Variation: Create a more hearty soup by adding 2 cooked, sliced potatoes.

Minestrone

⅓ cup kidney beans
¾ cup noodles and macaroni shells
3 carrots
1 small onion
1 stalk celery
1 large potato
4 tablespoons olive oil
½ pound (1–2 medium) tomatoes or
   ½ medium (16-ounce) can tomatoes
5 cups vegetable stock
½ teaspoon Miso or Tamari Soy Sauce
Salt
1 bay leaf
1 tablespoon marjoram, finely chopped
2 cloves of garlic, crushed or
   1 tablespoon garlic granules
¾ cup grated Parmesan cheese
2 teaspoons chives, finely chopped
1 tablespoon parsley, finely chopped

Wash and soak the beans in a large pot covered with water for at least 12 hours, longer if possible. Bring them to a boil in the same water, cover, and reduce the heat and simmer until soft, about 2 hours. Boil the noodles in a covered saucepan with 2 cups of salted water until soft, about 15–20 minutes. Wash, peel, and cube the vegetables. Heat the oil in a large saucepan, sauté the carrots for 2 minutes, then add the celery, onions, and potatoes. Sauté for 10 more minutes, stirring all the while. Add the tomatoes and half the stock, cover, and simmer gently until all the vegetables are tender. Now add the cooked beans, noodles, the water in which they were cooked, the rest of the stock, Miso, salt, bay leaf, marjoram, and finally the chopped garlic. Bring to a boil, then reduce the heat and simmer for ½ hour. Serve with plenty of grated cheese, chopped chives, and parsley on each plate.

Noodle Soup

2 tablespoons butter or margarine
5 cups vegetable stock
½ cup noodles
1½ teaspoons Miso or Tamari Soy Sauce
Salt
Chopped parsley

Add the butter to the stock in a covered saucepan and bring to a boil. Add the noodles and boil until they are soft (15–20 minutes). Add the Miso, salt, and parsley to taste.

Mulligatawney

2 shallots
2 carrots
2 leeks
1 turnip
2 stalks celery
6 tablespoons butter
4 cups stock
2 tablespoons white beans, or
    navy beans, cooked
1 small apple, finely chopped
¼ cup raisins
1½ teaspoons whole wheat flour
2 teaspoons curry powder
Sea salt
Large bay leaf
Lemon juice

Precook the beans in a covered saucepan with 1 cup of boiling, salted water until tender; drain. Peel and cut one shallot into 1-inch cubes; finely chop the other shallot and set it aside. Clean and cut the rest of the vegetables into 1-inch cubes. Sauté vegetables in 2 tablespoons butter in a saucepan for 8 minutes. Add half the stock, reduce the heat and simmer until the vegetables are very tender. Add the cooked beans, the remaining 4 tablespoons of butter, the other shallot, the apple, and the raisins. Simmer for 5 more minutes.

While the soup is still on low heat, mix the flour and curry powder together in a bowl, sprinkle into the soup, and stir for 1–2 minutes. Add the salt and bay leaf, cook for 2 minutes, then pour in the rest of the stock. Bring to a boil, cover, reduce the heat and simmer until the soup is thick and creamy, stirring occasionally. All the ingredients should now be blended. Simmer for 10 more minutes and serve. Drop in a little lemon juice at the last minute. For those who like a more fiery soup, add more curry powder.

Spring Soup

12 asparagus tips
1 cup hulled (1 pound unshelled) peas
2 small carrots, cut into matchstick pieces
1 large (17-ounce) can of sweet corn kernels
6–8 cups strongly-flavored vegetable stock
1 small tomato

Cook separately all of the vegetables, except the tomato, by steaming or boiling in a covered saucepan with a small amount of water until tender. Add the cooking water to the soup stock; however, add only 2 tablespoons of the asparagus water to the stock because of its strong smell. Skin and dice the tomato. Add all the cooked vegetables and tomato to the heated soup stock and serve.

Fresh Green Pea Soup

⅓ cup minced green onions
4 tablespoons butter
2½ pounds (2½ cups hulled) fresh peas
Salt and pepper
Dash of nutmeg (optional)
1 teaspoon honey
1 teaspoon fresh chervil
½ cup water
1 cup milk
Cream (optional)

Melt the butter in a deep frying pan and sauté the green onions until tender. Add the peas, seasonings, honey, nutmeg, chervil, and ½ cup water. Cover and simmer until the peas are tender. Purée in the blender with 1 cup of milk. Add more milk or cream to make a creamier soup. This can be served either hot or cold. If serving hot, heat the milk to just below boiling before blending.

Pea and Avocado Soup

⅓ cup green onions, minced
4 tablespoons butter or margarine
2 pounds (2 cups hulled) peas
½ cup water
Salt and pepper
1 teaspoon honey
1 avocado
1 cup milk or cream, or combination of both

Melt the butter in a saucepan, and sauté the green onions until soft. Add the peas, seasonings, water, and honey. Cover and simmer until the peas are tender.

Peel and mash ¾ of the avocado. Purée in the blender with 1 cup of milk and the cooked pea mixture. Add more milk or cream to make the purée like thick cream. Cut the rest of the avocado into very thin slices and serve as a garnish. This soup has a superlative flavor.

Potage aux Haricots Verts (Green Bean Soup)

½ pound fresh green beans
2 large potatoes
1 small onion
4 cups stock
4 tablespoons butter or margarine
5 tablespoons whole wheat flour
4½ tablespoons savory
Sea salt
½ teaspoon Miso or Tamari Soy Sauce
2 tablespoons cream
Chopped chives

Wash the vegetables, remove and discard the strings from the beans. Cut the green beans into diamond-shaped pieces. Peel and cube the onion. Boil the beans and potatoes in a large covered saucepan with the stock until soft. Strain and save the stock and vegetables in separate bowls. Mash and set aside the potatoes.

In a saucepan, sauté the onion in melted butter until it is lightly browned; add the flour and cook over low heat for several minutes. Pour in the stock; cook and stir over medium heat until slightly thickened. Now add the cooked beans, the mashed potatoes, the savory, salt, and Miso and simmer for 10 minutes. Add the cream just before serving and sprinkle with chopped chives.

Potato Soup

2 medium potatoes
2 large carrots
1 medium onion
2–3 stalks of celery
2–3 outer cabbage leaves
4 tablespoons butter or oil
4 cups vegetable stock or water
Salt and pepper to taste
1 teaspoon Miso or Tamari Soy Sauce
¼ teaspoon marjoram
Garnish of croutons

Wash the vegetables. Cut the cabbage leaves into very thin strips and cube the rest of the vegetables. Sauté the carrots in a large saucepan with 2 tablespoons of melted butter for 1 minute; add the celery, onion and cabbage and cook over very low heat for 10 minutes without water. Stir often so that the vegetables do not stick to the pan and burn. Add the potatoes and cook for 5 more minutes. Now add 1 cup of water or stock, cover, and simmer until the vegetables are nearly tender. Finally add the 3 remaining cups of boiling stock, 2 tablespoons butter, salt, pepper, Miso, and marjoram. Simmer for 5 more minutes until the vegetables are tender. Top with croutons made from whole wheat bread.

Potato and Leek Soup

4 large white potatoes
4 medium leeks, minced
1 large onion, minced
3 tablespoons butter or oil
Sea salt and pepper
1 cup water
3 cups milk
½ cup Half and Half
Garnish of chopped parsley

Boil potatoes in their skins in a saucepan with plenty of water until they are soft; then drain and cool. Trim and wash the leeks, using first a warm rinse and then a cold rinse. Mince the leeks with the onion and sauté together in a saucepan with the melted butter or oil. Peel and dice the potatoes and add to the leeks; add salt and pepper and sauté for 2 more minutes. Add 1 cup of water and simmer until all the vegetables are tender. Blend with 3 cups of milk in the blender, then stir in the Half and Half by hand. Serve hot or cold, garnished with parsley on each serving.

Sweet Potato Soup (Bisque)

1 pound (2–3 medium) sweet potatoes
2 cups stock, heated
2 tablespoons honey
Dash of nutmeg
½ cup cream
Sea salt
Sherry (optional)
Garnish of toasted almonds, roasted chestnuts
*   or walnuts*

Boil the potatoes in a saucepan with plenty of water until soft. Skin and mash the potatoes. Heat the stock in a large saucepan; stir in the potatoes, honey, nutmeg, and cream. Season to taste and top with sliced nuts.

Variation: For a luxurious soup add a spoonful of sherry in each bowl.

Rassolnik

5 tablespoons dill pickles, minced
2½ cups vegetable stock
8 very small beets
2 cups water
Salt and cayenne pepper
2 teaspoons honey
Lemon juice or vinegar (optional)
2 cups sour cream
4 inches of cucumber
2 hard boiled eggs
2 tablespoons fresh dill, finely chopped

Boil 2 eggs in a saucepan with plenty of water until hard boiled, 10–13 minutes. Drain, peel, slice, and chill the eggs. Peel the cucumber, cut into slices, and chill.

Soak the dill pickles in the stock while the rest of the soup is being made. Cut the beet stems into 1-inch lengths, wash the beets very carefully, and boil together in a covered saucepan with 2 cups of water for 20 minutes. Purée the beets with the beet cooking water in the blender. Season with salt and cayenne pepper, and add the honey. Add the pickles and stock, and if desired, a little lemon juice or vinegar. Chill to serve, spoon some sour cream into each bowl, add the soup and stir gently to barely mix it. Garnish with the chilled cucumber, egg, and dill.

Tomato Soup from the Garden

1½ pounds (2–4 medium) fresh ripe tomatoes
1 large onion, diced
4 tablespoons oil
2 tablespoons whole wheat flour
4 cups stock or
   2 cups stock mixed with 2 cups milk or
   4 cups milk
1 bay leaf
1 teaspoon honey
1 tablespoon lemon juice
Salt and pepper
Garnish of grated cheese

Cut the tomatoes and onion into bite-size pieces. Sauté the tomatoes and half the onions in a frying pan with 2 tablespoons of oil until soft. Purée in the blender. Sauté the remaining onions in a saucepan with 2 more tablespoons of oil until golden; add the flour, and cook over low heat for 4 minutes, stirring. Add the tomatoes and the stock you have chosen, and simmer until slightly thickened. Add the bay leaf, honey, lemon juice, and seasonings. Simmer for 10 more minutes, stirring often. If the soup starts to curdle, whisk it and it should settle down. Serve with grated cheese sprinkled on top.

Tomato Soup with Dill

½ cup onions, diced
3 tablespoons butter or margarine
5 cups tomatoes, skinned and chopped
Sea salt and pepper
1 teaspoon honey
2 tablespoons lemon juice
2 tablespoons fresh dill, minced
Garnish of chopped parsley and sour cream

Sauté the onions in a saucepan with melted butter for 3 minutes; add the tomatoes, and season with salt and pepper. Simmer for 15 minutes, then purée in the blender. Pour back into the saucepan and add the honey, lemon juice, and minced dill. Simmer gently for 5 more minutes. Serve hot or cold, garnished with sour cream and chopped parsley.

Thick Tomato and Celery Soup

1 bunch celery
2 large onions, sliced
2 carrots, diced
1 teaspoon Miso or Tamari Soy Sauce
Sea salt and pepper
2 cloves
½ teaspoon each of dried thyme, basil,
  and tarragon
4 tablespoons white wine or
  1 tablespoon vinegar
2 teaspoons honey
Stock or water
4 teaspoons arrowroot or cornstarch
1 medium (12-ounce) can of tomato purée or
  2 pounds (4–6) fresh tomatoes, skinned
  and puréed
Garnish of sour cream

Wash and thinly slice the celery, being sure to include some of the freshest green leaves. Put the celery, onions, and carrots in a thick saucepan with the Miso, seasonings, white wine or vinegar, and honey; cover with stock or water. Cover the pan and simmer for 1¼ hours. When the vegetables are really soft and tender, purée them in the blender or press through a sieve. Mix the arrowroot with a little of the tomato purée and add to the soup. Add the rest of the puréed tomatoes and simmer all together for 8–10 more minutes. Garnish each serving with a generous spoonful of sour cream.

Pepper and Tomato Soup

2 large red or green peppers
½ cup olive oil
2 pounds (4–5) tomatoes
2 teaspoons onion, grated
Sea salt and pepper
⅓ cup parsley, chopped

Preheat oven to 325°F
Bake the whole raw peppers for 25 minutes in the oven at 325°F. Put the peppers in a brown paper bag, place in a steam rack over a small amount of boiling water and steam for 5 minutes. Remove from the heat and discard the skin, fiber, and seeds. Cut the peppers into strips and marinate in olive oil for 1 hour. Skin and chop the tomatoes, then purée with the oil, peppers, onion, salt, and pepper in the blender. Garnish with parsley and serve hot or cold.

Variation: For a quick version of this soup: substitute a small can of tomato purée for the fresh tomatoes.

Quick Vegetable Soup

2 tomatoes
¼ small cabbage
1 carrot
Few sprigs of cauliflower
4 cups stock or water
1 small onion, diced
2 tablespoons butter or margarine
Sea salt
½ teaspoon Miso or Tamari Soy Sauce
Garnish of chopped parsley or chervil

Wash and dice all the vegetables, except the onion. Blend in the blender with the stock or water. Sauté the onion in melted butter in a saucepan until it is transparent. Add the blended vegetables, heat to the boiling point, then simmer for 20 minutes. Season with salt and Miso. Serve sprinkled with chopped parsley or chervil.

Vegetable and Squash Soup

2 cups (1–2 pounds) acorn squash
3 cups vegetable stock
Pinch of either ground ginger or mace
2 tablespoons honey
Sea salt and pepper
½ teaspoon Miso or Tamari Soy Sauce
½ cup Half and Half
2 tablespoons sherry

Peel and cube the acorn squash; then boil or steam in a saucepan with water until tender. Purée in the blender with a small amount of stock until smooth, then blend in the rest of the ingredients, except the sherry. If the soup is to be served cold, blend the sherry with the vegetables in the blender; place the soup in a bowl and chill in the refrigerator. If it is to be served hot, place the blended ingredients in a covered saucepan and heat over medium heat until just boiling. Remove from the heat, stir in the sherry, and serve.

Vichyssoise

4 large white potatoes
1 large onion
3 tablespoons butter
6 large leeks
Dash of nutmeg
Sea salt and pepper
½ teaspoon Miso or Tamari Soy Sauce
½ cup water
4 cups stock
1 cup milk
1 cup Half and Half
Garnish of chives

Peel and finely dice the potatoes and onion, place in a thick saucepan with the butter and sauté gently while you prepare the leeks.

Leaving on as much of the green as possible, trim, split, carefully wash, and cut the leeks into 6-inch lengths. Add the leeks, seasonings, Miso, and ½ cup of water to the potatoes and onion. Cover the pan tightly and simmer until tender. Purée in a blender, then mix with the stock, milk, and Half and Half. This soup is generally served cold with a garnish of chives. If the soup is too thick, thin it with milk or cream.

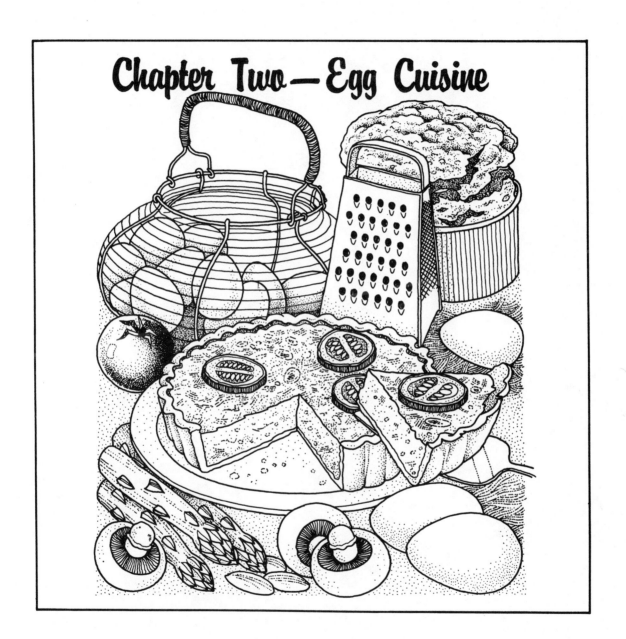

Chapter Two—Egg Cuisine

Chapter Two—Egg Cuisine

Eggs à L'Ardennaise

4 eggs
½ teaspoon mixed dry herbs (your choice of
   basil, oregano, tarragon, parsley, etc.)
Salt and cayenne pepper
3 tablespoons Half and Half

Preheat oven to 350°F

Separate the eggs. Beat the whites in a bowl
with an egg beater or whisk until very stiff, add
the mixed herbs, and season to taste with salt
and cayenne pepper. Pile the egg whites in
a greased shallow ovenware dish (9-inch
round or 9-inch square) and pour the Half and
Half over them. Make slight hollows and drop
the egg yolks in one at a time, making sure
they do not touch each other. Bake at 350°F
until the egg yolks are set, about 20–25
minutes. Serve at once from the dish.

Egg Nests

1¾ cups (2 medium) potatoes, mashed
4 eggs
Salt and pepper
¼ cup cheddar, swiss, or jack cheese, grated

Preheat oven to 350°F

If you do not have any mashed potatoes on
hand, boil 2 potatoes in a saucepan with plenty of water until soft; drain and mash. Put the
mashed potato in a 9-inch greased baking
dish and form it into four "nests", each one
large enough to take an egg. Break an egg
into each of the nests, sprinkle with salt and
pepper, cover with cheese and bake in the
oven at 350°F until the eggs are set, about
25–30 minutes.

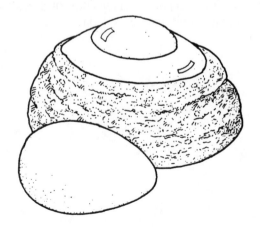

Parsley and Egg Fritters

Oil for frying
4 hard-boiled eggs
1 egg, beaten
Seasonings
Breadcrumbs
4 slices fried bread
Parsley, fried in a little oil

Cover the bottom of a frying pan with oil and heat over medium-high temperature as you peel and slice the hard-boiled eggs. Beat the egg in a small bowl. Season the breadcrumbs and place in another small bowl. Brush the hard-boiled eggs with the beaten raw egg, roll in the breadcrumbs, and fry in the very hot oil. Drain on paper towels and serve on slices of crisp fried bread or whole wheat toast. Garnish with fried parsley. Delicious for breakfast or for a snack later in the day.

Eggs à la Gruyère

4 ounces (1 cup) Gruyère cheese
½ teaspoon margarine
½ cup vegetable stock
Grated nutmeg
Sea salt
4 medium eggs (preferably fertile)
A little parsley and chives, finely minced

In a thick saucepan over medium-high heat quickly melt the cheese with the margarine so that the cheese does not have a chance to get stringy (as it will if it is over-heated). When melted, remove from the heat and add the stock, a pinch of nutmeg, and salt; mix well. Beat the eggs and herbs together, then blend into the cheese mixture. Fry in a frying pan with a little margarine or butter over medium heat until they reach the consistency of scrambled eggs. Serve with whole wheat toast.

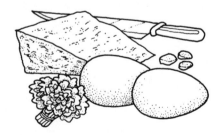

Egg and Cheese Timbales

2 tablespoons butter or oil
1 tablespoon whole wheat flour
1½ cups milk
½ pound (2 cups) cheddar, swiss, or
   jack cheese, grated
Salt
1½ teaspoons candied fruit mix (or jam)
1½ teaspoons chopped pimiento
3 eggs, beaten

Preheat oven to 350°F

Melt the butter in the top of a double boiler over hot water, slowly add the flour and milk, stirring constantly until thickened. Add the cheese and stir until it is melted. Remove from the heat, add the salt, fruit mix, and pimiento, and pour slowly into the beaten eggs, stirring all the time. Pour into 6 well-greased custard cups, place in a pan of hot water, and bake for 45 minutes at 350°F. See if they are done before the 45 minutes are up by sticking a knife in one of them; if it comes out clean, they are ready to eat. Remove from the cups and serve.

Cheese and Egg Crispies

4 eggs, beaten
1 tablespoon onion, grated, or
   a little garlic
1 tablespoon whole wheat flour
½ teaspoon salt
Good pinch of paprika
⅓ cup Gouda cheese, grated
1 tablespoon oil

Mix the eggs, onion (or garlic), flour, salt, paprika, and grated cheese in a large bowl. Heat the oil in a frying pan over medium heat until a drop of water makes it sizzle. Take a large spoonful of the egg mixture and drop it into the oil. Fry over high heat until brown on both sides, turning only once. Add more oil to the frying pan if the crispies start to burn or stick to the pan. Drain on paper towels and serve at once. Orange marmalade goes very well with these little crispies!

Egg and Tomato Delight

1½ pounds (3–4) tomatoes
1 clove garlic, finely chopped
1 teaspoon mint
1 teaspoon parsley
Salt and paprika
4 tablespoons olive oil
4 eggs
3 tablespoons Gouda cheese, grated
1 small (12-ounce) can tomato sauce

Peel, chop, and cook the tomatoes in a saucepan with the garlic, mint, parsley, and 2 tablespoons of the oil; simmer over low heat until the tomatoes are soft. Blend in the blender or press the mixture through a colander or sieve. Beat the eggs lightly in a bowl, add the cheese and tomato purée, then fry gently in a frying pan with the remaining 2 tablespoons of oil until set. Heat the tomato sauce until warm in a saucepan, and serve over the top of the eggs. Serve very hot.

Eggs with Port Wine

6 eggs
4 tablespoons butter
2 teaspoons shallots or green onions, finely chopped
1 tablespoon whole wheat flour
½ to 1 cup Port (to taste)
Pinch of mixed herbs
Sea salt and pepper

Boil the eggs until just hard (5–7 minutes) in a saucepan with plenty of boiling water, peel and cut each one in half lengthwise. Place in the top of a double boiler over simmering water to keep warm.

To make the sauce, sauté the shallots or onions in a saucepan with the melted butter for 2 minutes, add the flour, and stir over low heat until smooth. Add the port, salt, pepper, and herbs; bring to a boil, stirring constantly. Put the eggs on a warm dish, pour the sauce over top, and serve at once.

Soufflés

A soufflé is delicious and attractive and is not difficult to make; however, it must be eaten as soon as it is ready as it will "fall" if you delay!

Corn Soufflé

2 teaspoons whole wheat flour
1 teaspoon sea salt
4 teaspoons grated cheddar cheese
½ cup cream
4 egg yolks, well-beaten
1½ cups (1 large, 17-ounce can) sweet corn
1 little red bell pepper, de-seeded and diced
3 egg whites, stiffly beaten

Preheat oven to 350°F

Mix the flour, salt, and cheese together in a saucepan; and beat in the cream. Heat just to the boiling point, remove from the heat, and pour over the well-beaten egg yolks in a large bowl. Mince the corn and red pepper and add to the mixture. Beat the egg whites to a stiff peak stage, and fold in gently. Pour the mixture carefully into a greased soufflé dish. Bake 30 minutes at 350°F. Serve at once.

Carrot and Orange Soufflé

3 tablespoons melted butter or oil
3 tablespoons whole wheat flour
1 cup milk, heated
4 eggs, separated
Sea salt and pepper
1 heaping tablespoon raw onion, minced
2 large carrots, grated
1 heaping teaspoon orange peel, grated

Preheat oven to 350°F

Make a sauce in the top of a double boiler by slowly adding the flour and warm milk to the melted butter, stirring constantly. It is easier to make a smooth sauce if the milk is hot. Set to one side.

Add a little salt to the egg whites and beat in a bowl with an egg beater or whisk to the stiff peak stage, but not dry. Add the rest of the ingredients to the egg yolks in a large bowl and beat slightly; fold in the egg whites, and then pour the sauce into the mixture slowly, stirring gently. Season to taste and put into a lightly-greased casserole. Set the casserole in a pan of hot water and bake at 350°F for 50 minutes.

Lemon Soufflé with Lemon Sauce

SOUFFLÉ
3 tablespoons margarine
4 tablespoons flour
5 tablespoons milk
4 tablespoons honey
Rind of 1 lemon
4 eggs

SAUCE:
1½ lemons
1½ cups water
2½ tablespoons honey
2 teaspoons arrowroot or cornstarch
2 tablespoons cold water

Preheat oven to 375°F

SOUFFLÉ:
In the top of a double boiler, sift the flour into melted margarine. Stir well, add the milk, and then cook and stir for 5 minutes. Let cool a little, then beat in the honey and grated lemon rind. Separate the eggs and beat in the yolks one at a time. Beat the egg whites until a stiff peak forms when the beater is lifted; then fold into the first mixture with a metal spoon. Pour into a greased casserole or soufflé dish. Only fill half the dish as this soufflé rises to twice its original size. Bake for 30 minutes at 375°F.

SAUCE:
Grate the rind from the lemons and squeeze out the juice. Mix the rind, lemon juice, water, and honey together in a saucepan, and heat just to the boiling point. Blend the arrowroot with 2 tablespoons of cold water, and add to the boiling mixture. Cook and stir over low heat for 6–8 minutes. Serve hot with the soufflé.

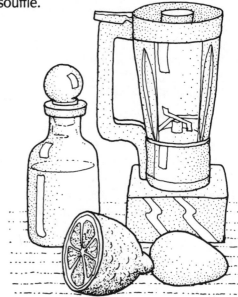

Onion Soufflé

SOUFFLÉ:
1½ pounds small onions
⅓ cup water
Salt and cayenne pepper
Pinch of cloves (optional)
4 tablespoons whole wheat flour
1½ tablespoons butter or margarine
½ cup cream
5 egg yolks, beaten
3 egg whites

TOMATO SAUCE:
1 small (12-ounce) can tomato sauce
1 pint sour cream

Preheat oven to 350°F

Peel and thinly slice the onions. Simmer in a saucepan with ⅓ cup of water, salt, pepper, and cloves until tender. Purée together in the blender. You should have 2 cups of onion purée.

Sift the flour into the melted butter in the top of a double boiler over hot water; stir in the cream. Cook and stir until thickened, remove from the heat, and add the beaten egg yolks. Beat well and add the onion purée. Beat the egg whites until very stiff and fold into the mix-ture. Pour into a greased soufflé dish or cas-serole and bake at 350°F for 25-30 minutes.

TOMATO SAUCE:
Heat the tomato sauce in a saucepan, remove from the heat and blend in an equal amount of sour cream. Serve hot on top of the soufflé.

Swiss Chard Soufflé

1½ cups (1–2 bunches fresh) chard
½ teaspoon dried thyme
Cream
1 cup liquid made from the chard
    cooking water and cream
2 tablespoons oil or margarine
3 tablespoons whole wheat flour
3 eggs separated
Salt and pepper

Preheat oven to 350°F
Wash the chard, separate the leaves from the ribs, and cut the ribs into 2-inch lengths. Cook the chard leaves and ribs together in a covered saucepan with ¼-inch of water over low heat for 10–15 minutes until not quite tender. Drain and keep the liquid; and purée the chard in a blender with the thyme.
In a saucepan, add enough cream to the chard cooking liquid to make 1 cup of stock, blend in the melted margarine, sift in the flour, and cook and stir over low heat until thickened. Remove from the heat, allow to cool slightly, then beat in the egg yolks. Mix together with the chard purée in a bowl, and season with salt and pepper. Beat the egg whites until stiff, then fold into the purée mixture. Place in a greased casserole or soufflé dish and bake for 40 minutes at 350°F. This soufflé should be a little soft inside.

Tomato Soufflé

1 tablespoon mild onion, grated
1½ tablespoons butter or margarine
1 cup tomato purée
Salt and pepper
Grated rind of 1 orange
1 cup orange juice
½ cup whole wheat flour
4 eggs, separated
Cream sauce (optional)

Preheat oven to 350°F

Sauté the onion in a frying pan with the melted butter until tender. Add the purée, salt, pepper, and orange rind; cook gently over low heat for 5 minutes. Remove from the heat and set aside. Blend the orange juice into the flour in a bowl; add the beaten egg yolks and mix well. Add to the tomato purée mix. Beat the egg whites until stiff and fold into the first mixture. Pour into a greased soufflé dish and bake for 25 minutes at 350°F. Serve with a cream sauce separately.

There are many different kinds of ingredients you can put into a soufflé. Use your imagination—just be certain they are not too heavy as the soufflé will "fall" if it is too heavy!

Curried Rice Soufflé

3 eggs, separated
1 cup dry white wine
1 cup Swiss cheese, grated
1 teaspoon prepared mustard
Pinch of cayenne pepper
½ teaspoon salt
2 teaspoons butter
1 teaspoon onion, grated
½ cup rice, precooked
1½ teaspoons curry powder
Salt and pepper
6 large individual soufflé dishes

Preheat oven to 400°F

If you do not have any precooked rice on hand, add ¼ cup rice to ¾ cups boiling, salted water in a covered saucepan, and cook over low heat 30–40 minutes until tender and dry. Be careful to not let it burn! Cool.

Lightly beat the egg yolks in a large bowl and set aside. Heat the wine in a saucepan until just simmering, and add the cheese, mustard, pepper, salt, butter, and onion. Stir over very low heat until the cheese is partially melted; then pour the mixture over the lightly beaten egg yolks in a large bowl. Mix the rice and curry powder together in a bowl and stir into the first mixture. Beat the egg whites to the stiff peak stage with an egg beater, fold gently into the mixture, and season to taste. Fill 6 greased soufflé dishes only ¾'s full. Bake at 400°F for 20 minutes or until the soufflés are puffed and golden brown. Serve at once.

Pea Soufflé with Almonds

2 pounds (2 cups hulled) green peas
Butter
3 tablespoons milk
2 tablespoons whole wheat flour
¼ cup toasted almonds, minced
½ cup cream
2 drops of almond or ratafia extract
3 eggs, separated
Salt and pepper

Preheat oven to 350°F

Hull and simmer the peas in a saucepan with a little water and butter until tender. Then mash, or blend in the blender, with the milk and flour. There should be 2 cups of purée.

Mix the almonds and cream in a saucepan and heat just to the boiling point. Remove from the heat, add the pea purée and extract, and beat in the egg yolks. Beat the egg whites to a stiff peak and fold into the first mixture, adding salt and pepper to taste. Turn into a greased soufflé dish and bake at 350°F for 30 minutes. Serve at once.

Soufflé Omelette

2 eggs
2 tablespoons hot water
Seasonings of salt, pepper plus your
    favorite herbs
2 tablespoons butter or margarine

Separate the yolks and whites of the eggs, and beat the whites in a bowl with an egg beater or whisk until stiff. In a separate bowl, beat the yolks well, add the seasonings and hot water, beat again, then fold into the egg whites. Melt enough butter to cover the bottom of an 8-inch frying pan completely. It is best to use a cast iron frying pan or omelette pan for this. Pour in the egg mixture and cook over moderate heat until the underside is a delicate light brown. Place the frying pan, as is, under the broiler to brown the top. Make a slash in the middle, fold the omelette over, and slip onto a hot dish. Serve without delay. Do not try to cook more than 4 eggs at once in this manner! Never try to put a heavy filling in a soufflé omelette—it is too delicate and cannot bear the strain.

Many variations can be made on this basic recipe so let your imagination lead you to try both sweet and piquant omelettes.

Breadcrumb Omelette

An inexpensive omelette may be made using breadcrumbs. It is suitable for breakfast or for an invalid on a light diet. Older people often find it easier to digest and less rich than more conventional omelettes.

4 medium eggs, separated
Salt and pepper
1 cup breadcrumbs
½ cup milk
1 tablespoon oil

Lightly beat the egg yolks in a bowl, then add the pepper, breadcrumbs, and milk. In a separate bowl, add a little salt to the egg whites and beat until stiff but not dry. Fold the whites into the yolk mixture. Heat the oil in an omelette pan over medium heat. Do not let it get too hot (smoking oil is too hot) or it will cause the eggs to be tough. Pour the omelette mixture into the pan and swirl it around the pan to spread it evenly. Put a lid on the pan and cook over low heat so that the bottom is lightly browned. Cook for 20 minutes, or until the surface is just dry to the touch. Fold over and serve plain or with a sauce of your choice (pages 121–123).

Asparagus Omelette

2 teaspoons arrowroot or cornstarch
⅔ cup Half and Half
Dash of nutmeg
Salt and cayenne pepper
Parmesan cheese, grated
5–6 eggs
3 tablespoons oil
8–10 (fresh or canned) asparagus tips, cooked

Make a sauce by blending the arrowroot and Half and Half in the top of a double boiler over boiling water; when well-blended, stir in the cheese, and season to taste. Cook and stir until thickened, cover, and keep warm over low heat.

If you are using fresh asparagus tips, steam them in a covered saucepan with a steam rack and ½ cup of boiling water until tender; drain and gently stir into the sauce in the top of the double boiler. Beat the eggs, a dash of Half and Half, salt, and pepper together in a bowl. Pour into a heated, well-oiled omelette pan and cook over medium heat until set. Put half the sauce on the cooked omelette, fold it once, and slip onto a hot dish. Pour the rest of the sauce on top and sprinkle with a little more cheese. Serve at once.

Broccoli Omelette

6 eggs, beaten
1 cup (½ pound) broccoli
1 tablespoon parsley, chopped
Salt and pepper
2 tablespoons onion, grated
¼ cup cream
3 tablespoons oil or margarine
½ teaspoon olive oil
Parmesan cheese, grated

Wash, chop, and steam the broccoli in a saucepan with a steam rack over boiling water until just tender; drain and finely chop. Mix the beaten eggs, cooked broccoli, parsley, salt, pepper, grated onion, and cream together in a bowl. Melt the margarine in an omelette pan and pour the egg mixture into it. Cook over moderate heat, lifting the edges so that it cooks evenly. When it is golden on the bottom but still slightly moist on top, fold over once and slip onto a heated dish. Pour ½ teaspoon of olive oil on top and sprinkle liberally with cheese.

Sweet Corn Omelette

2 tablespoons celery, minced
3 green onions, minced
2 tablespoons butter or olive oil
⅔ cup (fresh or canned) sweet corn, cooked
4 tablespoons cream, heated
Salt and cayenne pepper
6 eggs, beaten
Dash of cream
Parsley or chervil, chopped

If you are using fresh corn, boil the cobs in a covered saucepan with plenty of boiling water for 10 minutes until tender; drain and scrape the kernels off into a bowl with a knife. Melt the butter in a frying pan, and sauté the onion and celery until soft. Remove from the heat, add the corn, cream, salt, and cayenne to the onion mix, and stir well.

Beat the eggs in a bowl with a dash of cream, salt, and pepper; pour into a greased and heated omelette pan, and cook over medium heat until set. Fill the cooked omelette with the corn mixture, fold over, and serve at once. Garnish with chopped parsley or chervil.

Potato Omelette

1 cup (2 medium) potatoes, mashed
3 tablespoons butter
6 eggs
2 tablespoons cream
Salt and pepper
1 tablespoon oil
Chopped chives and sour cream as garnish

If you do not have any leftover mashed potatoes, boil 2 potatoes in a saucepan with plenty of boiling water until soft. Drain, mash, and season with salt, pepper, and your favorite herbs. Heat a tablespoon of butter in a frying pan, and fry the potatoes over medium heat until a light golden brown on both sides.

Beat the eggs, cream, salt, and pepper together in a bowl. Heat the butter and oil together in the omelette pan, pour in the egg mixture, and cook over medium heat until set. Spread the potatoes over the cooked omelette, fold once, and slip onto a hot dish. Garnish with sour cream and chives.

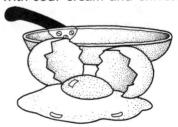

Spanish Omelette

Sauce:
¼ cup onion, minced
1 small green pepper, diced
3 large mushrooms, diced
2 tablespoons olive oil
3 black olives, sliced
2 teaspoons lemon juice
2 tomatoes, peeled and chopped

Omelette:
4–6 eggs
Salt and pepper
A little cream
1 tablespoon butter
Chopped parsley for garnish

Heat the oil in a saucepan and sauté the onion, green pepper, and mushrooms until tender. Add the rest of the ingredients for the sauce and simmer for 5 minutes.

Beat the eggs with a little salt, pepper, and cream in a bowl. Heat the butter in an omelette pan and cook the egg mixture over medium heat until set. When the omelette is set, but not dry, slip onto a dish, but do not fold. Cover with the sauce, garnish with chopped parsley, and serve.

Pumpkin Omelette

½ pound pumpkin
1 tablespoon of honey
4 eggs
Salt and pepper to taste
Margarine
Parsley as garnish

Peel and cut the pumpkin into very thin slices. Simmer gently in a covered pan with just enough water to cover the pumpkin; add a dash of salt and a tablespoon of honey. When tender, mash, and leave to cool. When cool, purée in the blender with the eggs and seasonings. Melt the margarine in a frying pan and pour in the omelette mixture. Cook over medium-high heat, lifting the mixture from time to time so that it does not burn. Slide the omelette onto a hot plate, roll or fold it and garnish with parsley.

Quiches

Quiches consist of a pie shell filled with an egg, cream, and vegetable mixture. Quiches are actually fairly simple to make and provide a hearty brunch or serve as an hors d'oeuvre.

Pie crusts work best if you freeze the butter first, then grate it into the flour. Use a pastry cutter to cut the butter into the flour until it is very fine, moisten with icy cold water and egg (optional) and stir until it reaches the right consistency. (The right consistency means it is moist enough not to crumble when you roll it out, and dry enough not to be a sticky dough.) The less you handle it, the lighter and flakier your crust will be.

Choose the pastry recipe you wish to use, mix all the ingredients together, press into a ball and roll out flat. Place into a pie pan. If the recipe you are using calls for a precooked shell, preheat the oven to 450°F and bake the shell for 10–12 minutes, or until lightly browned. Cool before filling. If the recipe does not require the pie shell to be precooked, make the pastry, line the pie pan, and place in the refrigerator until needed.

Basic Pastry #1

Makes one shell

1 cup whole wheat flour
8 tablespoons butter
Ice water
Pinch of salt

Basic Pastry #2

Makes one shell

½ cup whole wheat flour
½ cup rolled oats
8 tablespoons butter
1 egg
Ice Water

Basic Pastry #3

Makes one shell

½ cup whole wheat flour
½ cup flaked millet
8 tablespoons butter
1 egg
Ice Water

Basic Filling for Quiches

4 egg yolks
1 cup cream
Salt and pepper
Dash of nutmeg
Gouda cheese, sliced
Vegetables (optional), your choice,
cooked and chopped

Preheat oven to 375°F

Make a pie crust with one of the above recipes, line a pie pan, and place in the refrigerator until needed.

Prepare whichever vegetables you wish to use for the quiche filling. Some tasty options are: 2 medium sized onions cut in rings and sautéed in butter; ½ pound mushrooms, sliced and sautéed in butter; pieces of lightly cooked leeks, tomatoes or celery. The list is endless!

Beat the egg yolks, cream, salt, pepper, and nutmeg together in a bowl. Place slices of Gouda cheese on the bottom of the pie shell or grate into the egg mixture. Put the chosen cooked vegetable filling into the pie shell and pour the egg mixture on top. Bake at 375°F until the filling is set and brown on top, about 30–35 minutes. Serve hot or cold.

Chapter Three — Main Dishes

Chapter Three — Main Dishes

Jerusalem Artichokes au Gratin

Jerusalem artichokes have a "smoky" taste which blends well with cheese. They can be prepared in different ways—the following recipe is a simple but excellent dish.

1½ pounds Jerusalem artichokes
2 teaspoons arrowroot or cornstarch
Salt
1 cup Half and Half
1 tablespoon butter
Dash of nutmeg
½ cup cheddar or swiss cheese, grated

Wash, then simmer the Jerusalem artichokes in a saucepan with 1 cup of water until tender (approximately 20 minutes). Drain, keeping 3 tablespoons of the liquid for later use. Peel the skins and submerge the artichokes in slightly salted, cold water. Work quickly with the Jerusalem artichokes, as once they have been cut they will turn black with exposure to air.

Blend the arrowroot and Half and Half in the top of a double boiler over hot water; add the butter, seasonings, and 3 tablespoons of artichoke water that you saved. Cook, stirring constantly, until thickened. Drain the artichokes, mix with the sauce and place in a greased, shallow baking dish. Cover with cheese and broil for a few minutes until the cheese is melted and light brown in color.

Jerusalem Artichoke Pancakes

BASIC PANCAKE BATTER:
¾ cup flour
Pinch of salt
1 large egg
1 cup milk
PANCAKE FILLING:
1 pound Jerusalem artichokes
1 small onion, grated
1 large egg, beaten
¼ cup whole wheat flour
Salt
Oil for frying

Make the basic pancake batter first. Sift the flour and salt together into a bowl; make a well in the center and drop in the egg, add the milk slowly and stir until the batter is like thin cream. Do not beat because this makes the batter tough. Set aside for 10 minutes. Peel and grate the raw artichokes. Drain off the juice and mix quickly with the pancake batter and the rest of the ingredients, except the oil. Heat the oil in a frying pan and carefully pour the batter into pancake shapes. Fry over medium heat until golden brown on both sides. Serve hot.

Artichokes à la Roma

2 lemons
8 artichokes
1 cup parsley, chopped
¼ cup pennyroyal or peppermint, chopped
1 teaspoon salt
½ teaspoon white pepper
½ teaspoon garlic, finely chopped
¾ cup olive oil

Preheat oven to 350°F

Squeeze the juice of 1 lemon into a bowl filled with cold water. Remove the tough outer leaves of the artichokes, trim the stems to 1 inch, clip ¼-inch off the tops of the other leaves with scissors, and put the artichokes into the lemon water.

While the artichokes are soaking, mix the parsley, pennyroyal, salt, pepper, and garlic together in a bowl. Take the artichokes out of the water one at a time, pinch the stalks so that the leaves open out and push as much of the herb stuffing as you can into the spaces.

When all the artichokes are stuffed, place in a casserole dish, pour the olive oil over the top, and sprinkle with any leftover stuffing. Cover the bottom of the casserole with a little water, cover tightly, and bake for 1 hour at 350°F. Baste once or twice with the liquid from the dish. Serve hot.

Artichokes with Lemon Sauce

1 artichoke per person
Boiling, salted water
White wine, 2 tablespoons per artichoke
Olive oil, 2 tablespoons per artichoke
Salt and pepper
Lemon juice
French mustard
Capers (optional)

Wash the artichokes and remove the discolored leaves. Plunge into boiling, salted water and simmer for 5 minutes. Lift out of the water and drain upside down.

The following measurements are for six artichokes. Stand the artichokes upright and close together in a saucepan filled with ⅓ cup of white wine and ⅓ cup of olive oil. Sprinkle with salt and pepper. Separate the leaves a little and pour 2 tablespoons of olive oil and 2 tablespoons of wine in each artichoke. Cover tightly and simmer for 25–30 minutes until tender.

Sauce: Mix the juice of one lemon with 2 tablespoons each of mustard, wine, capers, and oil. Serve the sauce in individual bowls so that each leaf may be dipped into it.

Artichoke Hearts with Mushroom Sauce

12 or more artichokes, or canned artichoke
  hearts
¼ cup vegetable stock or water
¼ cup white wine
Salt and pepper
¾ cup (½ pound) mushrooms, sliced
1 tablespoon butter
2 teaspoons whole wheat flour
½ cup cream
Dash of nutmeg

Remove all the leaves and the hairy center or "choke" from each artichoke, leaving only the heart and stem. Peel each stem. If the hearts are very small use 2–3 for each serving. Place in a large saucepan, add the stock, wine, salt, and pepper. Cover and simmer for 15 minutes.

Melt the butter in a frying pan and lightly sauté the mushrooms, then add to the cooked artichoke hearts. Mix the flour with the cream and nutmeg in a bowl, stir until well blended, and pour over the artichokes. Simmer and stir gently for another 5–10 minutes until the sauce is thickened. If you are in a hurry, substitute arrowroot or cornstarch for the flour, as it works faster as a thickening agent. Serve at once.

Artichokes à la Grecque

6 large artichokes
1 lemon
1 onion, finely chopped
2 garlic cloves, crushed
¼ cup olive oil
3 stalks celery, minced
1 cup parsley, finely minced
½ cup (1 ounce) dill, finely chopped
1 teaspoon mint, finely chopped
Salt and pepper

Wash the artichokes well, clip ½-inch off the tops of the leaves. Trim the stems level with the bottom leaves. Squeeze the juice of 1 lemon over the artichokes and cook in a saucepan with boiling, salted water for 20 minutes. Drain and leave to cool. When cool, remove enough of the center leaves to scrape out the hairy section or "choke." Sauté the onion and garlic in a frying pan with 1 tablespoon of olive oil until soft; remove from the heat and mix in a bowl with the celery, parsley, dill, mint, salt, pepper, and remaining oil. Stuff the artichokes; place closely together in a large saucepan with water nearly covering them. Cook over low heat for 30 minutes. Serve either piping hot or chilled.

Asparagus Amandine

2½ pounds (2–3 bunches) asparagus
4 tablespoons butter, melted
½ cup sour cream
Salt and pepper
1 tablespoon onion, grated
⅔ cup almonds, finely chopped

Steam the asparagus in a covered saucepan with a steam rack over ½ cup of boiling water until tender; drain well, and place in a shallow baking dish. Mix the melted butter, sour cream, seasonings, and onion together in a bowl; then pour over the asparagus. Sprinkle the almonds on top and broil until the top is browned.

Hungarian Asparagus

2½ pounds (2–3 bunches) asparagus
1 cup sour cream
Salt and pepper
2 tablespoons lemon juice
½ cup fresh breadcrumbs
3 tablespoons oil or butter

Preheat oven to 400°F

Steam the asparagus until tender in a covered saucepan with a steam rack and 1 cup of boiling water. Drain well, and place in a shallow baking dish. Heat the sour cream, salt, pepper and lemon juice in a saucepan over very low heat until just warm; stir constantly or the sour cream will curdle. Pour over the asparagus. Melt the butter in a frying pan, and stir fry the breadcrumbs until golden brown; sprinkle over the asparagus. Bake at 400°F for 4 minutes or less.

Italian Asparagus

2½ pounds asparagus
2 cloves garlic, crushed
⅓ cup olive oil
Salt and pepper
1 tablespoon lemon juice
Parmesan cheese, grated

Steam the asparagus until tender in a covered saucepan with a steam rack and 1 cup of boiling water. Drain well, and place on a flat serving dish. Heat the garlic in a frying pan with the olive oil; season with salt, pepper, and lemon juice. Pour over the top of the asparagus and sprinkle a little cheese on top.

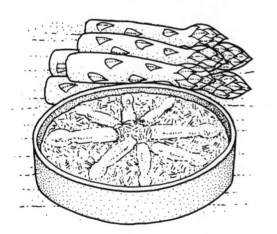

Asparagus Pie

1 pastry shell, precooked (page 44)
2½ pounds asparagus
2 tablespoons arrowroot or cornstarch
1½ cups Half and Half
Salt and pepper
2 egg yolks
2 tablespoons Parmesan cheese
Garnish of grated cheese

If you do not have a precooked pastry shell, make a pastry shell and bake.

Cut the asparagus tips into 4-inch lengths. Place in a saucepan, add enough salted water to barely cover the asparagus and simmer until tender. Drain and keep warm. In a saucepan, mix the arrowroot, Half and Half, and seasonings; cook and stir over low heat until thickened. Then add the egg yolks and cheese and continue to cook over low heat until the cheese just melts. Arrange half the asparagus in the baked pastry shell like the spokes of a wheel; add half the sauce. Put the rest of the tips on top and cover with the rest of the sauce. Sprinkle with Parmesan cheese and broil until the top is brown.

Beets in Orange Sauce

2 bunches small beets (preferably baby beets)
1 tablespoon vinegar
1½ tablespoons arrowroot or cornstarch
¾ cup orange juice
1 tablespoon orange rind, grated
Salt and pepper
⅛ teaspoon cloves, powdered
Juice of 1 lemon
3 teaspoons butter
Honey
Garnish of chopped chives

Scrub, then simmer the baby beets in a covered saucepan with 1½ cups of water with the vinegar (to keep the beets a rich red color). When tender, strain and keep the liquid; skin the beets and keep warm in the oven at 200°.

In a saucepan, blend the arrowroot with the orange juice, rind, pepper, salt, cloves, lemon juice, and butter; cook over low heat, stirring until thickened. Add ¼ cup of strained beet juice; taste. If it is too acid, add a little honey. Add the beets to the sauce, place in a shallow dish, and serve with chives sprinkled on top. If baby beets are not available, use large beets, but be sure to slice them.

Beets in Pomegranate Sauce

8 medium beets
1 tablespoon vinegar
½ cup pomegranate juice
1 tablespoon honey
1½ teaspoons arrowroot or cornstarch

Scrub, then boil the beets in a covered saucepan with 1½ cups of water with vinegar until tender. Drain and peel. Peel a pomegranate and squeeze through a sieve to extract the juice. Heat the pomegranate juice with the honey and arrowroot in a small saucepan. Cook and stir over low heat until thickened. Add the beets and serve hot.

Beets in Cranberry Sauce

2–3 bunches of baby beets
1½ cups cranberries
½ cup orange juice
2 tablespoons honey

Boil the beets until tender in a covered saucepan with plenty of water; drain and peel. Cook the cranberries in the orange juice in a saucepan over medium heat until soft, purée together in the blender, and strain through a sieve to remove the skins. Sweeten to taste; add the cooked beets, reheat over medium heat until hot, and serve. Try serving this with boiled or fried rice, or with a plain omelette.

Beets in Sour Cream

2 bunches of young beets
2 tablespoons margarine or oil
2 tablespoons lemon juice
Dash of nutmeg
1 tablespoon honey
2 tablespoons fresh onion juice (optional)
Salt and pepper
¾ cup sour cream
Garnish of chives or chervil

Preheat the oven to 400°F

Wash, then simmer the beets in a covered saucepan with 2 cups salted water until tender. Strain and keep the liquid. Peel and cube the beets, purée in the blender, adding some of the beet liquid if the purée becomes too thick to blend. Blend in the rest of the ingredients, except the sour cream. Put this purée in a baking dish and cover with the sour cream. Heat in the oven for 8 minutes at 400°F. Sprinkle with chopped chives or chervil as the dish is being served. This dish goes very well with poached eggs.

Beet Soufflé

6–8 baby beets
1½ tablespoons honey
Juice of 1 lemon
4 teaspoons fresh onion juice
Dash of powdered cloves
Salt and cayenne pepper
4 large eggs, separated
2 tablespoons arrowroot or cornstarch
½ cup orange or grapefruit juice

SAUCE:
Cooking water left over from the beets
Pinch of cloves
Pinch of salt
Honey to taste
1 teaspoon lemon or grapefruit juice
2 teaspoons arrowroot

Preheat oven to 350°F

Wash and boil the beets in a covered saucepan with 2 cups of water until tender. Drain and keep the liquid. Peel and dice the beets; then blend in the blender with the honey, lemon juice, onion juice, cloves, salt, and pepper. Beat the egg yolks together in a bowl; blend the arrowroot with the fruit juice in a separate bowl; blend both with the beet mixture in the blender. Beat the egg whites to a still peak and fold into the beet purée.

Pour the mixture into a greased 9-inch soufflé dish and bake at 350°F for 30 minutes. This soufflé should be moist inside.

SAUCE:
Mix all the sauce ingredients together in a saucepan and simmer over low heat, stirring until thickened. Serve in a sauce dish or gravy boat.

Beets Baked in Sour Cream

12 beets (the size of tangerines)
Salt and pepper
2 teaspoons lemon juice
2 teaspoons honey
1½ tablespoons margarine or olive oil
1 cup sour cream
Garnish of chopped chives or chervil

Boil the beets in a saucepan with 2 cups of water until tender. Drain and cool, then skin and slice the cooked beets. Stir together all of the ingredients in a saucepan; add the sour cream last. Simmer over low heat just until the mixture is heated through, but do not let it even begin to bubble or it will curdle. Serve sprinkled with either chives or chervil.

Broccoli Loaf

¼ cup onion, minced
2 tablespoons olive oil or melted margarine
2 pounds broccoli, fresh
2 tablespoons whole wheat flour
⅓ cup cheddar cheese, grated
2 eggs, beaten
1½ cups rice or bulgur, precooked
1 teaspoon oregano
Salt and pepper

SAUCE:
½ cup cream
Vegetable cooking liquid
2 teaspoons flour
Sherry
Cheddar cheese, grated
Mushrooms, sautéed

Preheat oven to 350°F

If you do not have any precooked rice, add ½ cup raw rice to 1½ cups boiling water, cover and simmer for 30–45 minutes until tender. Sauté the onions in a frying pan with the oil for 2–3 minutes. Coarsely chop the broccoli, steam 5–10 minutes in a covered saucepan with a steam rack and 1 cup water until tender, but still crisp. Drain, keeping the liquid for the sauce. Mix all the ingredients together and place in a greased bread pan.

Bake for 30 minutes at 350°.

SAUCE:
In a saucepan, blend ½ cup of cream and ½ cup of vegetable liquid, or water, with the flour. Simmer and stir until thickened. Add a little sherry, grated cheese and sautéed mushrooms. Serve in a gravy boat with the loaf.

Variation: Any leftover green vegetable or mixture of vegetables may be used for this loaf; cauliflower is good. If you use potatoes, omit the rice. Try substituting 2 cups of breadcrumbs for the rice.

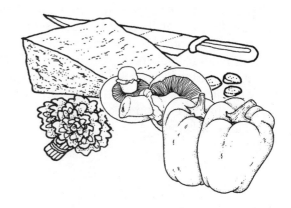

Broccoli Casserole

1 green pepper, sliced
¼ cup onion, diced
2 tablespoons margarine
2½ pounds broccoli
1 cup water
2 tablespoons arrowroot or whole wheat flour
1½ cups Half and Half
Sea salt and pepper
⅔ cup cheddar cheese, grated

Preheat oven to 425°F

De-seed, slice, and sauté the green pepper with the onion in a saucepan with melted margarine for 2 minutes. Slice the broccoli and add it with 1 cup of water to the green peppers. Cover tightly and simmer until just tender; drain. In a small saucepan, blend the arrowroot with the Half and Half. Simmer, stirring until thickened. Season with salt and pepper. Put alternate layers of vegetable and sauce in a casserole, with sauce on top. Cover with the cheese and bake at 425°F until the cheese is brown.

Brussels Sprouts with Chestnuts

15 chestnuts
1½ pounds small brussels sprouts
2 tablespoons butter or oil
2 tablespoons fresh onion juice
Vegetable stock or water
2 teaspoons arrowroot or cornstarch
Salt and pepper
Dash of nutmeg

In a saucepan, cover the chestnuts with boiling water, simmer 20 minutes, and drain. Remove the outer shell and inner skin while they are still warm. Cut the chestnuts into halves, and keep warm in the top of a double boiler over simmering water.

Wash and trim the brussels sprouts, removing all outer leaves. Simmer until tender in a covered saucepan with the butter, onion juice, and ½ cup salted water; drain and keep warm; keep the liquid. Add enough stock to the vegetable liquid to make 1½ cups of liquid. Blend the arrowroot with ½ cup of the stock; add to the total stock and simmer, stirring until thickened. Season with salt, pepper, and a dash of nutmeg. Add the heated chestnuts to the sauce, pour over the brussels sprouts, and serve.

Red Cabbage with Chestnuts

½ pound chestnuts
½ teaspoon butter
1 medium red cabbage, shredded
1 onion, diced
1 tablespoon margarine
¼ cup red wine
1 tablespoon honey
1 tablespoon arrowroot or cornstarch
½ cup cream
Dash of nutmeg
Salt and pepper

Stir fry the raw chestnuts over high heat in a frying pan with ½ teaspoon of butter until the chestnuts are well coated with the butter; then bake in a preheated oven at 350°F for 20–30 minutes, turning and watching for the skins to split. Remove both the outer shells and the inner, bitter skins while the chestnuts are still warm. Cut into halves.

Clean and shred the cabbage. Melt the margarine in a saucepan and sauté the onion for 1 minute, add the cabbage, wine, and honey; cover and simmer over low heat until the cabbage is just tender. Do not overcook. Drain, saving the juice. Stir the arrowroot into the cream in a saucepan until well blended; add the seasonings and blend by hand, or in the blender, with the liquid drained from the cabbage. Simmer over low heat, stirring until it thickens to a creamy consistency. Add the chestnuts, fold lightly into the cabbage, and serve very hot.

Sweet and Sour Cabbage

2 tablespoons butter
1½ pounds (1 small) green cabbage, shredded
Sea salt
Black pepper
2 tablespoons honey
2 tablespoons wine vinegar

Melt the butter in a large saucepan; add the cabbage, salt, and pepper and cover tightly. Cook over very low heat for 25 minutes. Add the honey and vinegar and continue to cook over low heat until the cabbage is tender. Check every once in a while to be sure it is not sticking to the pan and burning. Add a little water if the cabbage starts to stick. Serve very hot.

Variations: Add sliced apples and raisins. Substitute red cabbage and use red wine instead of vinegar. Serve with crispy noodles for a crunchy treat!

Chinese Cabbage—Chinese Style

1 Chinese cabbage (Bok Choy)
¼ cup soy or peanut oil
1 clove of garlic, crushed
½ teaspoon salt
1 tablespoon ginger root, minced
1 tablespoon arrowroot or cornstarch
1 tablespoon sherry
1 teaspoon soy sauce
Garnish of minced green onions

Wash and slice the cabbage into thin crosswise pieces. Put aside the loose leaf ends. Sauté the stalk and sliced leaves with stalk attached in a large frying pan, or wok, with the oil and garlic for 3 minutes over low heat. Then add the loose, tender leaves, salt, and ginger root. Sprinkle in a little water, cover and steam over medium heat until just tender. While the cabbage is steaming, blend the arrowroot with 2 tablespoons of cold water; then add the sherry and soy sauce and stir gently into the cabbage. Cook and stir over low heat for 3 more minutes and serve hot while the cabbage is still crisp. Garnish with green onions.

Baked Cabbage with Granny Smith Apples

1 small green cabbage
2 large sour cooking apples
½ cup unsweetened grapefruit juice
2 tablespoons margarine
1 cup sour cream
1 teaspoon chervil, minced
Salt and pepper

Preheat oven to 350°F

Grate the cabbage. Peel and grate the apples, and mix with the cabbage. Place in an 8-inch greased baking dish and pour the grapefruit juice over it. Cover with a tight lid of tin foil and bake for 30 minutes at 350°F.

In a small saucepan melt the margarine over low heat and blend in the sour cream and seasonings. Pour over the casserole, cover again and continue to bake at 350°F until tender. Season again to taste before serving.

Carrot Bake

1/4 cup vegetable oil
3 tablespoons whole wheat flour
Sea salt and pepper
1/2 teaspoon onion salt or grated onion
3 eggs, separated
2 cups (10–12 medium) carrots

Preheat oven to 350°F

Boil the carrots in a saucepan with plenty of water until tender; drain and mash. Heat the oil in a large frying pan, stir in the flour and lightly fry over medium heat until golden brown. Leave to cool for a second; then add the pepper, onion, slightly beaten egg yolks, and mashed carrots. Mix well. Add a little salt to the egg whites and beat them until stiff but not dry. Fold the egg whites into the carrot mixture. Pour into a greased bread pan and bake at 350°F for 30 minutes. Set a pan of hot water in the oven to keep the loaf moist. When done, remove the carrot loaf from the oven and let it stand for 5 minutes to cool. Remove from the pan and serve in slices on a hot platter. This is delicious served with a green salad!

Carrots Cooked in Stock

1 1/2 pounds (8–10) baby carrots
8 tablespoons butter or oil
2 teaspoons honey
Salt and pepper
1 teaspoon lemon juice
1 cup vegetable stock, white wine or water

Wash but do not peel the carrots, and cut into thin crosswise slices. Melt the butter in a thick frying pan, add the carrots, sprinkle with honey, salt, pepper, and lemon juice. Cover tightly and cook over very low heat, turning the slices over when they begin to brown. Add the stock and cover again. Cook until the carrots are tender and most of the stock has been absorbed.

Carrot Ring

2½ cups (10–13) carrots, boiled and mashed
1 cup Half and Half
5 teaspoons lemon juice
1 teaspoon prepared mustard
4½ teaspoons onion, grated
1½ tablespoons parsley, chopped
1 teaspoon salt
¼ teaspoon black pepper
2 tablespoons whole wheat flour
2 tablespoons margarine, melted
1¼ cups dry breadcrumbs
4 eggs, separated

Preheat oven to 350°F

Wash and boil the carrots in a covered saucepan with plenty of water until tender; drain and mash. Heat the Half and Half in a saucepan to just below the boiling point. Remove from the heat. Mix the mashed carrots with everything except the eggs. Beat the egg yolks and add them to the carrot mix. Beat the egg whites to the stiff peak stage and fold them in. Place the mixture in a greased and floured ring mold. Place a pan of hot water in the oven and stand the ring in it. Bake for 30–35 minutes at 350°F. Remove from the oven and leave to cool for 3 minutes before removing from the mold.

Variation: After baking, fill the middle with cooked green peas, or stewed tomatoes, or scrambled eggs.

Buttered Carrots with Herbs

8–10 (2 bunches) baby carrots
1 tablespoon lemon juice
1 tablespoon margarine
3 tablespoons water
Salt and cayenne pepper
Choose from the following herbs:
*   minced tarragon, parsley, green onions,*
*   chervil, basil.*

Wash the carrots and trim off the ends. Use the whole carrot if they are small and tender, otherwise cut into crosswise slices. Simmer for 10–15 minutes, or until tender, in a covered saucepan with the lemon juice, margarine, 3 tablespoons of water, salt, and cayenne pepper. Serve in a hot dish, adding more margarine to taste. Garnish with a generous sprinkling of herbs.

Carrots with Lemon or Orange Sauce

5–6 (1 bunch) young carrots
1 tablespoon lemon juice
½ cup water
Salt and pepper
2 tablespoons butter or margarine
2 teaspoons arrowroot or cornstarch
⅓ cup orange juice or
   3 tablespoons lemon juice
2 tablespoons honey
1 tablespoon parsley, minced

If the carrots are quite small, wash, trim off the root end, and use whole. If they are large, wash, and slice into lengthwise slices, or "chinese-cut" diagonal long slices. Simmer the carrots in a thick frying pan with the lemon juice, water, salt, pepper, and margarine. Drain, saving the juice. Put the carrots in a serving dish and keep warm in the oven at 200°F. In a saucepan add the arrowroot to the orange juice and stir until well blended. Sweeten with honey, add the liquid in which the carrots were cooked, then cook and stir over low heat until thickened. Pour over the carrots, sprinkle with parsley, and serve.

Carrot and Orange Soufflé

2 cups (10–12) carrots, boiled and mashed
2 tablespoons honey
Good dash of mace
Salt and pepper
¾ cup orange juice
4 green onions, minced
3 tablespoons arrowroot or cornstarch
Juice of ½ lemon
3 eggs, separated

Preheat oven to 350°F

Boil the carrots in a covered saucepan with plenty of water until tender; drain and mash. Heat the mashed carrots in a large saucepan over low heat with the honey, mace, salt, pepper, ½ cup of the orange juice, and the green onions. Stir the arrowroot into the remaining ¼ cup of orange juice and the lemon juice until well blended. Cook and stir over low heat until thickened. Blend both mixtures together in the blender with the egg yolks. Beat the egg whites until stiff and fold into the carrot mixture. Pour into a greased soufflé dish and bake at 350°F for 25 minutes. Serve immediately.

Braised Celery and Mustard

4 cups (12–14 stalks) celery, cut to 1-inch slices
3 tablespoons olive oil
2 tablespoons margarine
Salt and pepper
1 teaspoon dried fennel or basil
⅓ cup cream
1 tablespoon French mustard

Preheat oven to 400°F

Bake the celery with the olive oil, margarine, salt, pepper, and fennel or basil in an uncovered casserole dish at 400°F for 10 minutes; then lower the heat to 350°F and bake for 12 more minutes. If the celery is tough and old, extend the cooking time.

Blend the cream and mustard together in a saucepan; warm over low heat. Pour over the celery and serve.

Nutty Cauliflower Dip

1 cup nuts (any kind), chopped
½ pound cauliflower
4 tablespoons mayonnaise

Chop the nuts into little pieces. Wash and shred the cauliflower and mix with the nuts and mayonnaise. Use this dip with carrot or celery sticks for a tasty hors d'oeuvre.

Carrots, Apples, and Oranges

8 young carrots, shredded into long, thin slices
3 large sour apples, shredded
½ cup orange juice
Grated rind of 1 orange
8 tablespoons margarine, melted
Salt and pepper

Preheat oven to 325°F

Mix the shredded apples and carrots together in a shallow baking dish. Add the grated rind and orange juice; cover and bake for 35–40 minutes at 325°F until just tender. Season the melted margarine with salt and pepper, pour over the dish, and serve hot.

Celery with Nuts and Cream

1 medium-sized bunch of celery,
  cut into 2-inch lengths
Juice of ½ lemon
1 cup vegetable stock or water
Pinch of thyme
1 teaspoon golden syrup or honey
Salt and pepper
½ cup cream
⅓ cup cheddar cheese, grated
¼ cup mixed nuts or almonds, chopped

Preheat oven to 325°F

Arrange the celery on the bottom of a shallow baking dish. Squeeze the lemon juice over it; add the stock, thyme, and syrup. Bake at 325°F for 30 minutes. Drain and keep the liquid. Measure ½ cup of the reserved celery liquid into a saucepan; cook over low heat with the seasonings, cream, and cheese. As soon as the cheese melts, pour the sauce over the celery, sprinkle nuts on top and serve.

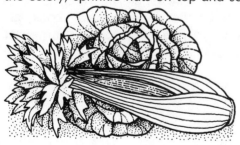

Creamed Celery au Gratin

⅔ cup leeks, minced
3 tablespoons oil or margarine
3 cups (10–11 stalks) celery, sliced
⅓ cup water
Salt and pepper
5 teaspoons arrowroot or cornstarch
Cream
¼ cup liquid stock made from
  celery cooking liquid plus cream
1 teaspoon curry powder
1 teaspoon turmeric
½ cup cheddar cheese, grated

Melt the margarine in a saucepan and sauté the minced leeks over low heat for 2 minutes. Add the sliced celery, water, salt, and pepper; cover tightly and simmer until the vegetables are tender. Drain and keep the liquid; put the celery into a shallow baking dish.

Add the arrowroot to ¼ cup of celery liquid; stir until well-blended. Add enough cream to the remaining celery liquid to make 1½ cups of liquid stock, then blend in the arrowroot liquid, curry powder, and turmeric; cook in a large saucepan over low heat until thickened. Pour over the celery, sprinkle the grated cheese on top and brown in a hot oven or under the broiler.

Swiss Chard Casserole

1½ pounds of cooked buttered chard
Cream
1½ cups of liquid stock made from
  chard cooking water and cream
1½ tablespoons arrowroot or cornstarch
½ pound mushrooms, sliced
½ cup shallots, minced
1 tablespoon butter
½ cup swiss cheese, grated

Preheat oven to 350°F

Prepare the chard using the recipe "Buttered Swiss Chard" (this page). Drain and keep the liquid. Add enough cream to the chard cooking water to make 1½ cups of liquid stock. Stir the arrowroot and liquid stock together in a saucepan and cook over low heat, stirring until thickened. Stir the sauce into the chard.

Sauté the mushrooms and shallots together in a frying pan with the butter for 5 minutes. Grease a baking dish or casserole and put in half the chard, cover with mushrooms and shallots; then add the rest of the chard. Cover and bake for 15 minutes at 350°F. Uncover, sprinkle with cheese, and bake for 10 more minutes.

Variation: Substitute breadcrumbs or cornflakes for the cheese to make a crunchier dish! Add 2 tablespoons of sherry to the sautéed mushrooms for a luxurious dish!!

Buttered Swiss Chard

1½ pounds (1–2 bunches) chard
1 mild onion or 6 green onions, minced
1 small green pepper, chopped
2 tablespoons olive oil
Salt and pepper
2 teaspoons lemon juice
½ teaspoon basil
¼ cup water

Wash the chard, then separate the leaves from the ribs; cut the ribs into 2-inch lengths. Sauté the onion and green pepper in oil in a thick saucepan for 1 minute. Add the chard ribs, sauté for 1 more minute, then add the leaves. (Cut or tear the leaves up, before cooking, if they are very large.) Add the salt, pepper, lemon juice, basil, and ¼ cup of water. Cover the pan and simmer over very low heat until the chard is tender (15–20 minutes). Serve very hot.

Baked Sweet Corn and Spanish Onions

Spanish onion per person
½ cup water
Dash of powdered cloves
Sea salt and pepper
2¾ cups (1 large 17-ounce plus 1 medium 8¾-ounce cans) cooked corn kernels

SAUCE:
1 cup liquid stock made from the onion cooking water and cream
2 tablespoons margarine, melted
4 teaspoons arrowroot or cornstarch
1 teaspoon turmeric
Grated cheese (your choice)

Preheat oven to 325°F

Cut the peeled onions into very thick slices and steam in a covered saucepan with ½ cup of water until tender. Do not let them become mushy by overcooking. Drain, keeping the liquid. Place the cooked onion slices in a greased baking dish, season with cloves, salt, and pepper; then cover with the corn. Keep warm in the oven at 250°F.

Add enough cream to the onion cooking liquid to make 1 cup stock. Melt 2 tablespoons of margarine in a saucepan, blend in the arrowroot, turmeric, and onion-cream liquid. Cook and stir over low heat until thickened. Pour the sauce over the onion-corn dish, sprinkle with cheese, and reheat in the oven until lightly browned.

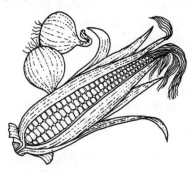

Sautéed Corn

2 large onions, thinly sliced
1 large green pepper, de-seeded and thinly sliced
4 tablespoons margarine
2 cups (2 medium 8¾-ounce cans) raw corn kernels
Salt, pepper, and paprika

Sauté the onions and green pepper in a large frying pan with the margarine until tender. Add the corn, stir gently, and sauté for 10 more minutes. Stir often or it will burn. Season and serve.

Sweet Corn Custard

3 tablespoons butter or margarine
1 teaspoon dried onion flakes, soaked
   in a little water
1 green pepper, de-seeded and diced
3 tablespoons raw corn kernels
Salt and pepper
Pinch of nutmeg
2 teaspoons honey
3 eggs, beaten
1¼ cups milk

Preheat oven to 350°F

Melt the butter in a frying pan, add the onion and green pepper, and sauté until tender. Remove from the heat and mix in a bowl with the corn. Season with salt and pepper; then stir in the honey, beaten eggs, and milk. Pour the mixture into a greased shallow baking dish and bake in the oven at 350°F until set (about 25 minutes).

Sweet Corn Pancakes

2 tablespoons whole wheat flour
1 teaspoon baking powder
½ teaspoon Sea salt
2 cups cooked corn kernels
   (2 medium 8¾-ounce cans)
1 cup milk or
   1 cup milk and sour cream mixed
2 eggs, separated
1 tablespoon butter or margarine

Sift the dry ingredients together; then mix in the corn, milk, and egg yolks. Beat the egg whites until stiff and fold into the batter. Heat an electric frying pan or thick frying pan as you would for pancakes, melt 1 tablespoon of margarine, and drop the batter onto it either from the tip of a spoon (if you want round pancakes) or from the side of the spoon (if you want oval pancakes). Fry on both sides until golden brown. Melt more margarine in the frying pan if the pancake batter starts to stick or burn. Makes about eight pancakes.

Corn Soufflé

2 teaspoons whole wheat flour
1 teaspoon Sea salt
4 teaspoons cheddar cheese, grated
½ cup cream
4 egg yolks, well-beaten
1½ cups sweet corn kernels
   (1 large 17-ounce can), drained
1 little red pepper, de-seeded
3 egg whites

Preheat oven to 350°F

Blend the flour, salt, and cheese in a saucepan; then beat in the cream. Heat just to the boiling point, then pour into a bowl over the well-beaten egg yolks. Mince the corn and red pepper and add to the mixture. Fold in the stiffly beaten egg whites. Pour the mixture carefully into a greased soufflé dish and bake at 350°F for ½ hour. Serve at once.

Sweet Corn Bake

12 ears of young sweet corn
1 cup cream
Salt and pepper
Nutmeg (optional)
2 tablespoons butter, melted
3 eggs, separated

Preheat oven to 300°F

Use the back of a large table knife to scrape all the kernels of corn and corn milk from the cobs into a large bowl; discard the cobs. Add the cream, and season with salt, pepper, and a dash of nutmeg. Stir in the melted butter and then the egg yolks. Lastly, fold in the stiffly beaten egg whites. Pour the mixture into a generously greased baking dish and bake for 35–40 minutes at 300°F. Then raise the heat to 375°F and brown the top for 5–10 minutes. Serve hot or cold.

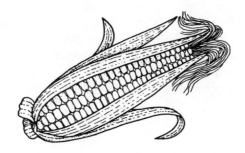

Dill Dumplings with Tomato Sauce

DUMPLINGS:
1 cup whole wheat flour
½ teaspoon salt
1 heaping teaspoon baking powder
1 teaspoon margarine
1 teaspoon cooking fat or oil
3 tablespoons fresh dill leaves, finely chopped
Milk

TOMATO SAUCE:
1½ tablespoons butter
3 tablespoons onion, sliced
2 cups tomato juice
Salt and pepper
Garnish of chopped parsley

Sift the dry ingredients for the dumplings together in a large bowl; add the margarine, oil, and dill. Mix well; then slowly stir in enough milk to make a soft, but not sticky, dough. Roll the dough into a big ball, flatten out on a floured surface and cut into nine pieces. Roll each piece into a ball, dust with flour, and chill in the refrigerator for 12 minutes.

Sauté the onions in butter in a saucepan until soft; add the tomato juice, salt, and pepper. Bring to a boil, then drop in the dumplings and boil for 12 minutes. Serve the dumplings covered with the sauce, garnished with chopped parsley.

Cream of Corn Delicious

3 tablespoons butter or margarine
1 tablespoon onion, grated
3 tablespoons green or red pepper, minced
1 large (17-ounce) can corn kernels
½ teaspoon salt
Black pepper
1 cup Half and Half
3 eggs, separated

Preheat oven to 350°F

Melt the butter in a large frying pan, add the onion and minced pepper, and sauté until the onion becomes transparent. Add the rest of the ingredients, except the egg whites. Beat the egg whites to the stiff peak stage and fold in. Pour into a greased soufflé dish and bake at 350°F for 15 minutes.

Yummy Dolmas

WRAPPING:
Grape vine leaves
½ cup seasoned vegetable stock (page 11)
¼ cup olive oil

STUFFING:
1 cup brown rice, precooked
¼ cup green onions, minced
¼ cup olive oil
1½ cups walnuts, minced
1 egg, beaten
Sea salt and pepper
1 teaspoon oregano
6 mint leaves, minced
½ cup raisins
3 tablespoons parsley, chopped
½ teaspoon cinnamon
3 teaspoons honey
1 teaspoon thyme
½ cup pine nuts (pignolias)

Preheat oven to 325°F

If you do not have any precooked rice on hand, add ⅓ cup raw rice to ⅔ cup boiling water, cover and simmer for 30–45 minutes until tender. Blanch the vine leaves in boiling water for 5 minutes, then drain. Sauté the onions in the olive oil in a frying pan until soft; then mix all the stuffing ingredients together in a bowl. Put 2–3 tablespoons of the stuffing on each vine leaf and roll up from the stalk ends, tucking the sides in as you roll.

Put the little rolls close together in a covered baking dish; pour ½ cup seasoned stock and ¼ cup olive oil over them; cover tightly and bake at 325°F for 1 hour.

You can make a sauce from the strained liquid in the baking dish, though it will need to be thickened slightly by adding 2 teaspoons of arrowroot or flour and cooking over low heat for a few minutes, stirring continuously.

Variation: Serve with tomato sauce, sour cream, mushroom or mustard sauce. If dolmas are made very small, they make good appetizers.

Real dolmas are always rolled in grape vine leaves; however, if you cannot buy vine leaves, substitute cabbage leaves. After blanching the cabbage leaves, cut away the thick ribs from the leaves, before rolling in the stuffing.

Eggplants

Some people find eggplants a little bitter. There are two ways to draw the bitterness out. One is to slice the eggplant, sprinkle it with a little salt, and let it sit for a while. Rinse. The other way is to slice and lightly fry the eggplant before baking.

Eggplant Provencale

2 eggplants
½ pound tomatoes (1–2 tomatoes)
1 small onion
3 tablespoons oil
Garlic salt or 1 clove garlic
Salt and cayenne pepper
Garnish of chopped parsley

Wipe the eggplants, but do not wash or peel. Cut into 1-inch cubes. Cut the tomatoes into halves. Peel and cut the onion into rings. Heat the oil in a large frying pan; add the garlic and onion rings, and sauté for 6 minutes. Add the tomatoes and eggplant cubes; sauté gently until tender. Serve, garnished with parsley.

Eggplant with Yogurt à la Turque

3 cloves garlic
2 cups yogurt
1½ pounds eggplant (1–2 medium eggplants)
½ cup whole wheat flour
Olive oil for frying
Sea salt and pepper

Make the yogurt sauce first as it must be served cold with the hot cooked eggplant. To make sauce: crush the garlic to a pulp, blend in a small bowl with the yogurt, and chill.

Wipe the eggplants off with a towel; then cut into ½-inch thick crosswise slices. Dust with flour and fry 4–5 slices at a time in moderately heated olive oil, ⅓ of an inch deep. Turn once. Remove from the oil when golden brown on both sides, drain on paper towels, and sprinkle with salt and pepper. Serve hot with the cold yogurt sauce on the side.

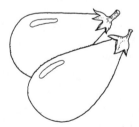

Eggplant Caviar

2 garlic cloves, crushed
3 tablespoons olive oil
1 medium eggplant
2 tablespoons green onion tops, minced
Salt and pepper
1 teaspoon cardamon powder
1 teaspoon powdered coriander seeds
Garnish of black olives

Preheat oven to 350°F

Soak the crushed garlic with the olive oil in a small bowl. Wipe and bake the eggplants whole and unpeeled for 40–60 minutes, according to size, at 350°F. Test for tenderness with a fine skewer or knitting needle. Leave to cool, then peel; discard the skin, and mash the eggplant to a pulp. Beat in the rest of the ingredients, including the garlic-olive oil. Serve with crackers as an appetizer, garnished with black olives.

Eggplant Baked with Herbs

1 large eggplant, sliced in ½-inch
  crosswise slices
Choice of oregano, thyme, tarragon, or basil
Salt and pepper
Oil for frying
Garnish of bran or grated Cheddar cheese

Preheat oven to 375°F

Since eggplants absorb a lot of oil while they cook, some people find them too rich and like to season slices of raw eggplant, and then brown them rapidly in very little oil over high heat.

Sprinkle the herb you have chosen for seasoning onto the slices before cooking. Fry in a small amount of oil until brown; then place in a shallow baking dish. When all the slices have been browned, bake in the oven at 375°F for 20 minutes or until tender. Sprinkle with bran or grated cheese.

Chinese Eggplant

1 large or 2 small eggplants
4 tablespoons sesame or peanut oil
Salt and pepper
2 teaspoons arrowroot or cornstarch
3 tablespoons cold water
2 teaspoons honey
2 teaspoons soy sauce
1 tablespoon preserved or
    candied ginger, minced
Green onion, chopped

Preheat oven to 350°F

Peel and cut the eggplant into ½-inch slices; discard the end pieces. Heat the oil in a heavy frying pan; lightly fry the slices over medium-high heat until brown; then sprinkle with salt and pepper. Place in a shallow baking dish and bake in the oven at 350°F until tender (about 15 minutes).

In the top of a double boiler blend the arrowroot with 3 tablespoons of cold water; add the honey and soy sauce; cook and stir until thickened and well-blended. If the sauce becomes too thick to stir, thin it with a dash of water or oil. Spoon the sauce over the tender eggplant, sprinkle with ginger and chopped onions, and serve.

Variation: Substitute very small squash or zucchini for the eggplant.

Baked Whole Eggplant

1 very large or 2 small eggplants
2 teaspoons basil
2 tablespoons olive oil
Butter
Salt and pepper

Preheat oven to 350°F

Mix the basil and olive oil together, season with salt and pepper. Wipe the eggplant; cut and discard a thin slice off each end. Place in a baking dish with a lid; make 4 lengthwise slashes on one side, and fill with the herb mix. Dot with butter in each slash. Cover the dish with a tight lid and bake at 350°F for ½ hour. Remove the lid, pour a dash of oil into the slits, cover and continue to bake until tender. Large eggplants take 1 hour, smaller ones take ½ to ¾ hour. Test for tenderness with a skewer or knitting needle. Slice in half to serve.

Eggplant and Noodle Bake

2 cloves garlic, crushed
⅓ cup olive oil
1 small eggplant
1½ cups shell noodles
1 teaspoon dried fennel
½ cup tomato sauce, fresh or
  canned (pages 70, 123)
Salt and pepper
¼ cup breadcrumbs
¼ cup grated Parmesan cheese

Preheat oven to 375°F

Crush the garlic and let it soak in a bowl with the olive oil while preparing the eggplant and noodles. Peel, cube, and steam the eggplant until tender in a covered saucepan with ½ cup boiling water. While it is steaming, add the noodles to 4 cups of boiling, salted water; boil for 7–8 minutes and drain. Do not overcook the noodles. Stir the garlic-olive oil into the noodles and place in a baking dish with the eggplant. Add fennel to the tomato sauce, season with salt and pepper, and stir into the eggplant mix. Top with breadcrumbs and Parmesan cheese. Bake in the oven at 375°F for 10 minutes.

Eggplant Pancakes

1 large eggplant
5 tablespoons whole wheat flour
  (approximately)
½ teaspoon baking powder
½ teaspoon Sea salt
2 tablespoons green onion tops or
  chives, minced
Olive or vegetable oil for frying

Wipe and cut the eggplant into slices. Steam the slices in a covered saucepan over 1 cup of boiling water for at least 10 minutes. When the eggplant is tender, peel and discard the skin; mash the pulp with a fork, but do not make it a liquid. Use 1 tablespoon of flour per 1 cup of eggplant pulp. Mix the flour, baking powder, Sea salt, and onion together; then stir gently into the pulp. Heat 1 tablespoon of oil until very hot in a frying pan, spoon the mixture into oil and fry over high heat until both sides have been browned; then turn down the heat to low and cook for 3 more minutes until the pancakes are cooked all the way through. This recipe makes about 12 small pancakes.

Eggplant, Tomato, and Zucchini Casserole

1½ pounds (3-4 medium) tomatoes,
    red and yellow mixed
2 teaspoons basil
1 teaspoon tarragon
1 tablespoon honey
Salt and pepper
¼ cup olive oil
2 garlic cloves, crushed
1 small eggplant, sliced
½ pound (3 medium-sized) unpeeled
    zucchini, sliced
2 large onions, sliced
1 green pepper, sliced

Preheat oven to 375°F

Skin and slice the tomatoes and either press them in a strainer to drain off some of the juice, or salt them and leave in a colander to drain for a few minutes. Dice the tomatoes, place half in the bottom of a greased casserole dish, and sprinkle with half the herbs, honey, salt, and pepper. Heat the olive oil with the garlic in a frying pan over low heat; then sauté, one at a time, the eggplant, zucchini, onion, and green pepper. Do not cook them all at once. Place all of the sautéed vegetables on top of the tomatoes in the casserole and season with the rest of the herbs, honey, salt, and pepper. Cover with the remaining half of the tomatoes and bake in the oven for 20 minutes at 375°F, then lower the heat to 350°F and bake for 20 more minutes until tender.

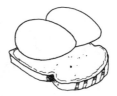

French Toast

6 slices of bread
1 teaspoon vanilla extract
2 tablespoons honey
6 tablespoons milk
Pinch of salt
3 egg yolks, lightly beaten
Margarine

Remove the crusts from the bread. Blend the vanilla and honey with the milk in a large bowl. Dip the bread slices in the milk, but do this quickly or the bread will either break or be too soggy. Add salt to the beaten egg yolks and dip the slices of bread into the egg yolks. Heat the margarine in a frying pan and fry the slices in it over medium heat until golden brown on both sides. Serve at once with honey or syrup.

Creamed Eggplant

2 eggplants
2 tablespoons butter
⅓ cup whole wheat flour
1 cup Half and Half
2 tablespoons grated cheddar cheese
Salt and pepper
1 teaspoon marjoram

Preheat oven to 350°F

Bake the whole eggplants in the oven at 350°F until tender (1 hour for large eggplants, ½ hour for small to medium ones). Make the sauce while they are baking. Melt the butter in a saucepan over medium heat, add the flour; cook and stir for 10 minutes. Stir in the Half and Half slowly and, when the sauce is smooth, add the cheese and continue to stir over low heat until the cheese is melted. Season with salt, pepper, and marjoram. If the sauce seems too thick, do not despair; all will be well because the juice from the eggplants will thin it! Peel and mash the cooked eggplants, then mix with the sauce. Serve with boiled brown rice to make a complete meal.

Frittata Verdi

½ cup spinach, chopped
1 tablespoon water
2 tablespoons parsley, chopped
2 tablespoons chervil, chopped
Salt and pepper
4 eggs, beaten
1 tablespoon cream
1 tablespoon spinach water
1 tablespoon grated Parmesan cheese
3 tablespoons olive oil

Wash the spinach thoroughly and steam until tender in a covered saucepan with 1 tablespoon of water (5–10 minutes). Drain and keep the water. Mix the spinach, herbs, and seasonings. Use fresh herbs whenever possible. Beat the eggs in a bowl, add the cream, spinach water, and cheese; beat again. Mix this gently with the spinach. Heat the oil in a frying pan and fry the egg-spinach mixture over a fairly high heat, lifting the side a little to allow the uncooked part to run underneath. When cooked and set, but not dry, place the frittata verdi in a round serving dish; do not fold over. Sprinkle with cheese and serve.

Gnocchi di Semolina

2 cups milk
½ cup semolina flour
3 tablespoons butter
1 egg yolk, beaten
⅛ teaspoon salt
Oil for frying
¾ cup grated Parmesan cheese

Preheat oven to 350°F

Bring the milk to a boil in a thick saucepan; then sift in the semolina a little at a time, stirring constantly with a wooden spoon. Lower the heat to medium when it begins to thicken; continue to stir and cook for 10 more minutes. Remove from the heat and add 1 tablespoon of butter, the egg yolk, and salt. Beat and stir vigorously; then pour onto a slightly damp marble slab or kitchen table top. Roll out the dough to ¾-inch thickness and leave to cool for at least 1 hour. Then cut with a sharp knife into little squares. Place the squares of gnocchi ¼-inch apart in a large, shallow, well-oiled ovenware dish. Sprinkle with the Parmesan cheese, dot with butter, and repeat the layers. Bake in the oven at 350°F until pale brown on top. Serve with a favorite sauce.

Herb Bread

1 loaf of French bread
1 tablespoon fresh herbs mixed
  (parsley, chives, marjoram, thyme, or chervil)
5 tablespoons margarine

Preheat oven to 425°F

Cream the margarine with the minced herbs in a bowl. Cut the French bread diagonally in ½-inch slices, but do not cut through the bottom crust. Spread each slice with some of the herb margarine. Press the loaf into shape again and wrap with tin foil. Put in the oven and bake at 425°F for 15 minutes. This is also delicious with just butter and garlic powder mixed together and spread on the bread.

Herb Scones (Biscuits)

⅔ cup self-rising flour
4 tablespoons butter
2 tablespoons chosen herbs (your choice of
   basil, tarragon, thyme, dill)
Pinch of salt
Milk to mix

Preheat oven to 425°F

Finely cut the butter into the flour until well mixed; add the herbs and salt, and stir in enough milk to make a soft dough. Roll the dough out to ¾-inch thickness on a floured surface. Cut into circles using a wine or drinking glass as your cutting shape. Place on a greased cookie sheet and bake in the oven at 425°F for 10–12 minutes until golden on the outside and cooked on the inside. Serve hot and buttered. These scones are very good placed on top of vegetable stews instead of dumplings.

Hoppity John

2 cups dried beans (any kind)
1 onion
Salt and pepper
5 cups cold water or vegetable stock
1 cup uncooked rice
2 cups water
2 teaspoons lemon juice
2 tablespoons butter
Salt

Soak the beans in a large bowl covered with water for 24 hours; then drain and place in a large thick saucepan with the onion, salt, pepper, and 5 cups of cold water or stock. Bring to a boil, cover and simmer over medium heat for 2 hours until the beans are tender. Lift out the onion and drain off all the water. In another saucepan, mix the rice, 2 cups of water, lemon juice, butter, and salt (to taste); bring to a boil and stir once with a fork. Cook at a medium heat, uncovered, for 20 minutes until the rice is dry and fluffy. Mix the rice and beans, add a tablespoon of butter or margarine, and season to taste. Simmer the complete mixture for 10 minutes and serve.

Kale with Cheese Sauce

1½ pounds curly kale
½ cup onion, minced
A little butter or margarine
Salt and pepper
2 teaspoons lemon juice
2 tablespoons water

SAUCE:
2 teaspoons butter or margarine
4 teaspoons whole wheat flour
½ cup Half and Half
1 cup grated cheese (your choice)

Wash the kale, remove the stems, and cut the leaves into bite-size pieces. In a saucepan sauté the onion with the butter for 2 minutes; then add the kale, salt, pepper, lemon juice, and 2 tablespoons of water. Cover tightly and simmer over low heat until tender. Drain and keep the liquid.

SAUCE:
Melt the margarine in a saucepan, stir in the flour, and cook and stir over low heat until it bubbles; then blend in the Half and Half and continue to cook over low heat until thickened. Add the grated cheese and liquid drained from the kale; cook and stir until blended. Put the kale and sauce into a greased baking dish and sprinkle thickly with cheese. Broil to melt and brown the cheese. Serve hot.

Leeks and Brown Rice

1 cup uncooked brown rice
2 cups vegetable stock (page 11)
3 large or
* 6 small leeks, minced*
3 tablespoons butter or margarine

Cook the rice in the seasoned stock for 45 minutes in a covered saucepan over very low heat. Sauté the minced leeks with the butter in a frying pan, then stir into the rice and leave to stand on the stove but without heat for 10 minutes to "blend" the flavors. This is a good side dish with a plain omelette.

Braised Leeks in Vegetable Stock

2 pounds (5–6 medium-sized) leeks
2 tablespoons butter or margarine
Salt and pepper
½ cup vegetable stock (page 11)
2 teaspoons arrowroot or cornstarch
3 teaspoons lemon juice
2 teaspoons cold water
Garnish of parsley or chervil

Trim off the roots of the leeks and remove some of the outer leaves, which will be tougher than the inner ones. Wash the leeks twice, using warm water for the first rinse and cold water for the second rinse. If the leeks are large, split them down the middle.

Put the leeks, butter, salt, pepper, and stock in a thick saucepan; cover and simmer over low heat until the leeks are just tender, about 10–15 minutes according to age and size of leeks. Blend the arrowroot with the lemon juice and 2 teaspoons cold water; add to the leeks and cook over low heat until the juice thickens to a creamy consistency. Place the leeks and sauce in a hot serving dish, sprinkle with parsley or chervil, and serve. Leeks cooked this way are especially tasty served over toast.

Leeks and Noodles

6 medium leeks, cut into ½-inch pieces
3 tablespoons butter or margarine
Salt and pepper
¾ pound (3 cups) shell macaroni or
  ribbon noodles
Boiling water
Grated cheese

Melt the butter in a frying pan, add the leeks, and sauté over low heat until soft. Season with salt and pepper. Boil the noodles in plenty of lightly salted water for 7 minutes, or until tender. Drain and mix with the leeks and serve covered with cheese.

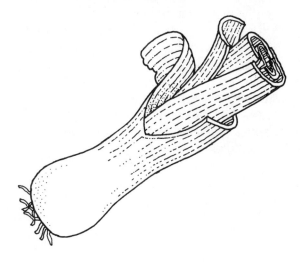

Creamed Leeks

2 pounds (6 medium-sized) leeks
2 tablespoons butter
¼ cup vegetable stock or water
½ cup cream
2 teaspoons arrowroot or cornstarch
Salt, pepper, and paprika
Grated cheese (optional)

Trim the roots and tips of the leeks, leaving as much green as possible. Wash them well and, if they are large, split them into halves. Melt the butter in a saucepan, add the leeks and sauté over low heat until soft. Add the stock, cover with a tightly fitting lid, and cook gently over medium-low heat until the leeks are just tender. In a small saucepan blend the arrowroot with the cream; add salt and pepper and cook and stir over low heat until thickened. When the sauce is thickened and smooth, place the leeks in a serving dish, cover with sauce and sprinkle lavishly with paprika. Serve with grated cheese on the side if you like.

Leeks with Lemon Sauce

2 pounds (6 medium-sized) leeks
3 tablespoons butter or margarine
2–3 tablespoons water
3 tablespoons lemon juice
Salt, pepper, and paprika
¾ teaspoon arrowroot or cornstarch
1 tablespoon water
Slices of buttered toast
Garnish of 2 hard-boiled eggs

Clean and trim the leeks; split into halves if they are large. Melt the butter in a large frying pan, add the leeks and sauté for 5 minutes. Add 2–3 tablespoons of water, the lemon juice, salt, pepper, and paprika. Cover and cook gently over low heat for 8 more minutes or until just tender. Blend the arrowroot with a tablespoon of cold water and stir into the leeks. Cook until the juice thickens into a sauce. Serve the leeks on top of slices of buttered toast and spoon the sauce over them. Peel and mash the hard-boiled eggs and sprinkle over the top.

Leeks Baked with Tomatoes

6 leeks
3 tablespoons butter or margarine
4 large, ripe tomatoes
Salt and pepper
Dash of basil
2 teaspoons arrowroot or cornstarch
½ cup cream

Preheat oven to 375°F

Wash and trim the leeks, then cut into 1-inch lengths. Bake in a shallow baking dish with the butter for 5 minutes at 375°F. Skin and cut the tomatoes into crosswise halves. Arrange on top of the leeks and sprinkle with a little salt, pepper, and basil. Bake in the oven at 375°F for 5 more minutes; then turn the tomatoes over and bake until all the vegetables are tender. Blend the arrowroot with the cream. Lift the tomatoes onto a hot dish and pour the arrowroot and cream over the leeks. Season and cook over medium heat until the sauce has thickened. Lift the leeks out and arrange attractively on the dish with the tomatoes; cover with sauce.

Leek and Potato Pie

2 large white potatoes
1 small onion
¼ cup water
Salt and pepper
3 tablespoons cream
Butter or margarine or olive oil
Browned breadcrumbs
2 cups leeks, minced
1 egg, beaten
1 cup sour cream

Preheat oven to 375°F

Peel and dice the potatoes and onion, and place in a covered saucepan. Cover with ¼ cup of water; season with salt and pepper; boil until tender. When cooked, drain and mash with cream and some butter or oil. Cover the sides and bottom of a greased, shallow pie pan with breadcrumbs; spread the potato mixture on top as if it were a pastry lining. Wash and trim the leeks; then sauté with butter or oil in a frying pan for 5 minutes or until just tender. Season with salt and pepper and spread on top of the potato mixture. Beat the egg into the sour cream, season and spread on top of the leeks. Bake in the oven at 375°F until the cream is a pale primrose color. Serve at once.

Stuffed Lettuce Leaves

Large lettuce leaves
Boiling water
1 cup (½ pound fresh) mushrooms,
  minced and sautéed
1 tablespoon butter
½ cup breadcrumbs
1 cup brown rice, precooked
1 egg, beaten
3 tablespoons sherry
4 tablespoons cream
½ cup parsley, minced
3 tablespoons chives, finely minced

Preheat oven to 350°F

If you don't have precooked rice on hand, then before starting this recipe add ⅓ cup raw rice to ⅔ cup boiling water, cover and simmer for 20–30 minutes until tender. Dip the lettuce leaves in boiling water for not more than 2 minutes and drain. Sauté the mushrooms in a frying pan with 1 tablespoon of butter, then mix in a bowl with the breadcrumbs, cooked rice, egg, sherry, cream, parsley, and chives. Put a little of this mixture on each lettuce leaf and roll up the leaf into little parcels with the ends tucked in, and fasten shut with toothpicks or string. Place the rolls close together in a greased baking dish; bake in the oven for 20 minutes at 350°F, then lift them out very carefully and serve on a heated serving plate with the liquid from the pan poured over the top.

Mushrooms with Artichoke Hearts

8 large mushrooms
½ cup olive oil
8 large artichoke hearts (canned or fresh)
¾ cup breadcrumbs, finely chopped
1 clove garlic, finely chopped
4 tablespoons parsley, chopped
Salt and cayenne pepper

Preheat oven to 325°F

Do not peel the mushrooms unless they are dirty and black; just wipe them with a damp cloth and scoop out the caps. Save the mushrooms and stalks that you scoop out. Heat ¼ cup of olive oil in a frying pan, add the mushroom caps and artichoke hearts, and sauté over low heat for 8 minutes. Stir gently so as not to break the vegetables. Sauté, in another frying pan with ¼ cup of olive oil, the breadcrumbs, chopped mushroom stalks, garlic, and parsley for 8 minutes. Arrange the artichoke hearts on a greased baking dish and cover each one with a mushroom cap, gills up. Fill the mushrooms with the breadcrumb mixture, sprinkle with salt and pepper, and bake in the oven for 10 minutes at 325°F.

Mushrooms with Madeira

¾ pound (25–30 medium-sized) mushrooms
2 cups milk
3 bay leaves
Cayenne pepper and salt
½ cup Madeira
2 teaspoons olive oil
2 teaspoons whole wheat flour

Wash, but do not peel the mushrooms, unless they are dirty. Cut the stalks even with the caps. Dice the stalks and add them to the milk and bay leaves in a saucepan; season with salt and pepper. Bring the milk to a boil, add half the Madeira and remove from the heat. In the top of a double boiler, heat the olive oil and stir in the flour; cook and stir for 10 minutes. Then slowly strain the milk into it, stirring and cooking until it thickens. If the mushrooms are button mushrooms, use them whole; if they are large, cut them into bite-size pieces. Add the mushrooms to the sauce and cook gently for 10–15 minutes; taste for seasonings and add any needed. (Some cooks like to add a little mace or nutmeg at this point.) Add the rest of the Madeira and cook over direct low heat until the sauce is thick. Pour into individual dishes and serve with thin slices of brown toast.

Stuffed Mushrooms

8 very large mushrooms
1 pound mixed size mushrooms
1¼ cups breadcrumbs
8 tablespoons margarine
2 shallots, chopped
2 tablespoons parsley or chervil, chopped
½ cup white wine or cream
Cayenne pepper and Sea salt
1 egg
Juice of 1 small lemon
Margarine

Preheat oven to 350°F

Peel the large mushrooms, cut off the stalks, scoop out the inside of the caps, and set aside. Wash and finely mince the rest of the mushrooms and stalks. Soak the breadcrumbs in just enough water to moisten them. Melt the margarine in a saucepan, add the chopped shallots, sauté for 5 minutes. Add the minced mushrooms, breadcrumbs, parsley or chervil, wine or cream, pepper, and salt. Cook over low heat for 8–10 minutes until the mixture looks drier. Remove from the heat and beat in the egg and lemon juice.

Arrange the 8 large mushrooms on a greased baking dish, pile the stuffing on them, and dot with margarine. Bake in the oven at 350°F and watch carefully. Take out of the oven as soon as they look browned on top (8–15 minutes, depending on the size of the mushrooms).

Nut Cutlets

4 tablespoons vegetable oil
5 tablespoons whole wheat flour
2 cups vegetable stock, slightly heated
Salt to taste
Any herbs, to taste
1 teaspoon Miso or Tamari Soy Sauce
¾ cup fine breadcrumbs
½ cup nuts, finely chopped
1 raw egg
2 tablespoons milk
Oil for frying

Heat 4 tablespoons of vegetable oil in a thick frying pan, add the flour, cook and stir for 2 minutes over low heat. Add the stock, salt, herbs, and Miso. Cook and stir for 10 minutes over medium heat; taste, and if the taste is "raw," continue to cook for a few more minutes. Remove from the heat and add ½ cup of the breadcrumbs and all of the nuts. Set aside to cool, then form into cutlets. Beat the egg and milk together in a bowl. Place the remaining breadcrumbs on a plate. Heat 1–2 tablespoons of oil in a frying pan over medium heat. Dip the cutlets in the egg-milk, then roll in the remaining breadcrumbs and fry until both sides are golden brown.

Nut Roast Loaf

½ pound (1–2 medium-sized) tomatoes
2 shallots
2 cups walnuts, slivered or finely chopped
1 teaspoon oil
2 eggs
Salt to taste
1 teaspoon chopped parsley and chives

Preheat oven to 400°F

Peel and dice the tomatoes. Skin and chop the shallots. Mix the walnuts, tomatoes, and shallots together in a bowl with 1 teaspoon of oil. Beat together the eggs, salt, and herbs; add to the walnut mix and blend. Put the mixture in a well-greased bread pan and bake in the oven at 400°F for 30–40 minutes. It should be well risen and golden brown when done. Serve on a heated serving dish, piping hot. Serve with any sauce you like on the side (See page 122 for sauces.)

Nut Rissoles

Rissoles are triangular or crescent shaped delectables!

4 tablespoons lentils
4 cups water
½ cup nuts, minced
2 cups breadcrumbs
2 eggs
Salt
Marjoram and thyme to taste
Flour
2 tablespoons milk
Oil for frying

Soak the lentils overnight in a large covered saucepan with 4 cups of water, then cook on medium-high heat in the same water until soft. Drain and mix the lentils with the nuts, breadcrumbs, 1 egg, salt, and herbs. Leave to stand for 30 minutes, then roll the dough out on a floured surface and cut into little rissoles (triangular shapes). If the dough is too wet and sticky, add more breadcrumbs.

In a separate bowl, beat the second egg and milk together. Dip the rissoles into the egg mix and then into the breadcrumbs. Leave for a few minutes to dry. Heat 2-inches of oil in a deep frying pan. When the oil is very hot, deep fry the rissoles until golden brown. Be careful not to splash the hot oil! Drain on paper towels and serve.

Spinach with Nuts

½ pound (1 bunch) spinach
3 teaspoons lemon juice
2 level teaspoons honey
1¼ cups nuts, grated
4 tablespoons mayonnaise

Wash the spinach well, shake off as much water as possible, and finely chop. Discard the stems. Mix with all the other ingredients, adding the mayonnaise last. Pile in a dish and refrigerate. Serve nice and cold!

Onion Quiche

PASTRY:
10 tablespoons whole wheat flour
5 tablespoons margarine
Pinch of Sea salt
Water

FILLING:
2½ cups onions, thinly sliced
2 tablespoons butter
Salt and cayenne pepper
Dash of powdered cloves (optional)
2 large eggs
2 teaspoons whole wheat flour
1 cup sour cream

Preheat oven to 375°F

Make the pastry shell first by cutting the margarine into the flour and salt in a large bowl until it is very fine and well-blended. Stir in enough cold water to make the dough bind together, roll out on a floured surface and place in a greased pie shell. Refrigerate.

Sauté the onions in a thick frying pan with the butter, salt, cayenne pepper, and cloves for about 20 minutes, until they are just tender. Spread the onions evenly in the pie shell. Beat the eggs and flour together, add salt; then mix in the sour cream and pour on top of the onions. Do not stir it in. Trim the pastry edges and bake in the oven at 375°F for 15 minutes; then turn the heat down to 325°F and bake for a further 8 minutes until the pastry is golden and the filling set. Serve hot.

Green Onions and Brown Rice

1½ cups uncooked brown rice
2 cups vegetable stock or water
1 teaspoon turmeric
3 tablespoons raisins
4 tablespoons sherry
2 tablespoons pine nuts (pignolias)
1 tablespoon preserved ginger, minced
½ cup green onions, minced

Put the rice in a saucepan with the stock and turmeric, cover and cook over low heat for 45 minutes. Soak the raisins in the sherry while the rice is cooking. Turn off the heat under the rice mixture and leave to stand covered for 10 more minutes. Add the raisins, nuts, ginger, and onions to the rice mix and stir. This dish may be served with scrambled eggs or on its own.

Onions Madère

1½ pounds small yellow onions
2 tablespoons honey
2 tablespoons butter or margarine
Pinch of mace
Salt and pepper
⅓ cup Madeira
4 tablespoons raisins
2 tablespoons currants

Preheat oven to 350°F

Peel the onions; use whole if bite-size or cut into bite-size pieces. Heat the honey and butter together in a frying pan over low heat, add the onion and cook, turning the onions until they are completely covered with the honey-butter and well-glazed. Put the onions in a shallow baking dish and sprinkle with mace, a dash of salt and pepper, Madeira, raisins, and currants. Cover tightly and bake in the oven for 40 minutes at 350°F. Look at the dish after 20 minutes and if a lot of juice has run out of the ingredients and gathered in the bottom of the dish, leave the cover off for the last 20 minutes of baking.

Onions Smothered with Almonds

1¼ cups whole blanched almonds
36 small onions
4 tablespoons butter or margarine
1 tablespoon honey
1 teaspoon salt
Pinch of cayenne pepper and nutmeg

Preheat oven to 350°F

Blanch raw almonds by soaking them in a bowl with boiling hot water for 2 minutes, drain, and pop off their skins. Bake in the oven on a cookie sheet at 350°F for 5 minutes to dry them out.

Wash and peel the onions. Melt the butter over low heat in an ovenware dish with lid; add the almonds; season with honey, salt, cayenne pepper, and nutmeg; blend carefully, then add the onions and stir until covered with the mixture. Cover the dish and bake in the oven at 350°F for 1 hour. Shake the dish frequently. The onions should be very tender and almonds golden brown.

Stuffed Crêpes

Crêpes are just very thin pancakes. They work best by using a thin batter and a very hot frying pan. Expect to throw away the first few crêpes as you learn how to swirl the batter around in the pan and how to flip it without breaking and cook without burning!! Don't give up; although they are tricky, they are also delicious!

¾ *cup whole wheat flour*
½ *teaspoon salt*
2 eggs
1 cup milk
1 tablespoon cooking oil

6-inch skillet or crêpe pan

Sift together the flour and salt in a bowl; drop in the eggs, stir, then add the milk and oil and stir just to blend. Beating the batter makes tough pancakes; any little lumps will disappear in the cooking. Leave the batter to stand for ½ hour or longer. Grease the bottom of the frying pan and place on medium-high heat. When the frying pan is hot pour in 2 tablespoons of batter, and swirl it around to spread it evenly on the whole pan. Flip only once after you see the pancake forming little bubbles on top. Keep hot in the oven at 200°F. When all the pancakes are cooked, fill each one with the chosen filling, roll up and put close together in a baking dish. Cover with either sauce or grated cheese and brown lightly under the broiler.

Any stuffing is good; sweet stuffings make a first class sweet treat! For a tasty filling try spinach and egg cooked together; sautéed mushrooms; soft cheese; tomatoes; cream cheese; boiled and chopped onions, or fried onions; leeks; asparagus and cheese sauce; fruits; and so on. Let your imagination run free!

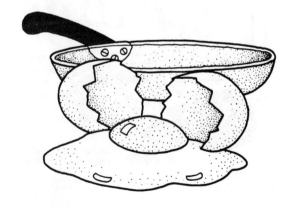

Pancakes

The great objection to making pancakes is that they leave such a strong smell of hot oil behind them that can permeate the whole house. The remedy is simple: just add a little oil to the pancake batter. After doing this, grease the frying pan once only for the first pancake and no more.

Basic Pancake Batter

¾ cup flour
Pinch of salt
1 large egg
1 cup milk
1 tablespoon oil

Sift the flour and salt together into a bowl; make a well in the center and drop in the egg, add the milk slowly and stir until the batter is like thin cream. Do not beat because this makes the batter tough. Set aside for 10 minutes; stir once and put into a jug. Just before using, add 1 tablespoon of oil to the batter and stir; this eliminates the need to keep greasing the frying pan. Use a frying pan about 6–7 inches in diameter. Grease the bottom of the frying pan and place over medium-high heat. When the pan is hot, pour in some batter and swirl it around to fill the pan about ¼-inch thick. When the top of the pancake begins to bubble, flip the pancake. Cook until both sides are golden brown.

There are all kinds of ingredients you can add to the basic mix such as raisins, nuts, and jams. The following recipes are some delightful variations. If the pancakes are to be stored, use just the basic recipe.

Sweet Corn Pancakes

5 tablespoons whole wheat flour
1 teaspoon baking powder
½ teaspoon Sea salt
2 cups cooked corn
1 cup milk or
½ cup milk and ½ cup sour cream mixed
2 eggs, separated

Sift the dry ingredients together in a bowl, then stir in the corn. Add the milk and egg yolks; stir until blended. Beat the egg whites until stiff and fold into the batter. Heat an electric frying pan or a thick frying pan over medium-high heat; grease the bottom of the pan with a little margarine and drop the batter onto it from the tip of a spoon (if you want round cakes), or from the side of the spoon (if you like oval ones). Fry until golden on both sides. Makes about 8 pancakes.

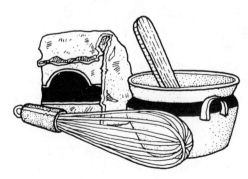

Eggplant Pancakes

1 large eggplant
½ teaspoon baking powder
½ teaspoon Sea salt
2 tablespoons green onion tops, minced
5 tablespoons whole wheat flour
   (approximately)
Olive or vegetable oil for frying

Wipe and cut the eggplant into quarters. Place the cut side down in a steamer over boiling water, cover and steam for at least 10 minutes. When it is tender, peel and discard the skin, slice the eggplant into a bowl, discard any juice, then mash the pulp with a fork. Mix the baking powder, Sea salt, green onion, and flour together in a bowl (use 1 tablespoon of flour per 1 cup of eggplant pulp) and blend into the eggplant. Heat a dash of oil in a frying pan over medium-high heat. When hot, pour in the eggplant batter and fry until both sides have been browned; then turn down the heat and cook the pancakes through (3–4 minutes).

This recipe makes about 12 small pancakes.

Nutty Stuffed Pancakes

PANCAKE BATTER:
⅔ cup flour
Sea salt
1 egg
1 cup milk

STUFFING:
1 cup white sauce (page 121)
2 large tomatoes, skinned and chopped
2 tablespoons oil
½ teaspoon garlic or onion salt
Pinch of Sea salt
3 tablespoons breadcrumbs
½ cup grated nuts

Sift together the flour and salt in a bowl; make a hollow in the middle and drop in the egg and ½ cup of milk. Beat well; then stir in the rest of the milk. Heat a little oil in a 9-inch frying pan. When the oil is hot, pour in small amounts of batter, swirl around and fry over medium heat until brown on both sides. The mixture will make 8 pancakes. Keep the pancakes hot in the oven at 200°F.

Make a white sauce if you don't have any on hand. Sauté the chopped, skinned tomatoes in a large frying pan with 2 tablespoons of heated oil, onion salt and a pinch of Sea salt. Cook gently for 5 minutes. Stir in the bread-crumbs and nuts. Cook over medium heat just enough to heat through; then blend in the white sauce. Spoon the mixture onto the center of each pancake and roll. Serve very hot. Grated cheese may be served on the side, or sprinkled on top of the rolled pancakes.

Jerusalem Artichoke Pancakes

1 pound Jerusalem artichokes
1 small onion, grated
1 large egg, beaten
¼ cup whole wheat flour
Salt
Oil for frying
PANCAKE BATTER:
⅔ cup whole wheat flour
1 egg
Sea salt
1 cup milk

Make the pancake batter first, using the above ingredients, following the basic pancake recipe (page 92).

Peel and grate the raw artichokes, drain off some of the juice, and mix quickly with the rest of the ingredients, except the oil. Blend into the pancake batter. Heat a little oil in a frying pan until hot, pour in the batter, and fry over medium heat, cooking both sides until golden brown. Serve very hot.

Potato Pancakes #1

1 pound (2 medium-sized) raw potatoes, grated
2 tablespoons of leftover mashed potatoes
2 tablespoons milk
2 eggs
1 teaspoon onion, grated
Salt and cayenne pepper
Oil
Honey
Schnapps or kirsch, heated

Mix the first six ingredients together in a bowl. Pour ½-inch of oil into the bottom of a deep frying pan and heat. When the oil is hot, spoon the potato pancake mix in, and fry over medium heat until golden brown on both sides. Drain on paper towels. Now comes the surprise! Put the pancakes on a hot dish, dab with honey, then "flambe" with the heated schnapps or kirsch. Be generous with the spirit!

Potato Pancakes #2

2 cups (5–6) white potatoes
2 tablespoons parsley, chopped
1 cup soft breadcrumbs
1 small onion, grated
2 eggs, beaten
4 teaspoons milk
½ cup cream

Mix all the ingredients together in a bowl in the order given. Form into small pancakes and roll in crumbs. Heat ⅛-inch of oil in the bottom of a frying pan. When the oil is hot, add the pancakes and fry until brown on both sides. Serve with one of the ready-made nut rissoles.

Parsnip Pie

Pre-made pie shell (page 44)

Melted shortening
1 pound (3 medium-sized) parsnips
1 pound green peas, hulled
1–2 medium potatoes
1 cup cream
4 teaspoons arrowroot or cornstarch
2 tablespoons onion, grated
Dash of mace
½ cup vegetable stock or water
Salt and pepper
Grated Parmesan or cheddar cheese for top

Preheat oven to 400°F

Make pastry from any of the pastry recipes on page 44 and line a 9-inch pie pan. Set aside enough pastry dough to make a lattice covering for the top. Brush the pie shell with melted shortening to keep from becoming soggy when filled, and bake in the oven for 15 minutes at 400°F.

Steam or boil the parsnips and peas separately in ¼ cup salted water. Save the parsnip and pea water for the sauce. Cook the potatoes in 2 cups boiling water. When tender, drain and cut into 1-inch cubes. Peel the parsnips. Make a sauce by blending together in a saucepan the cream and arrowroot; cook and stir over low heat until thickened; add the onion, mace, vegetable water, salt, and pepper. Continue to cook until well-blended and thick.

Arrange the vegetables in the pie shell and pour the sauce on top. Make a lattice of pastry strips over the top of the filling. Bake in the oven at 400°F until just brown. Serve hot with grated cheese on top.

Glazed Parsnips

6 large parsnips
2 tablespoons butter or oil
2 tablespoons orange juice
3 tablespoons honey
Salt and pepper

Wash, but do not peel the parsnips, then steam or boil in a covered saucepan with ¼ cup of salted water. Cook until tender, then skin and cut in halves lengthwise; if very long, cut crosswise as well. Heat the butter or oil in a thick frying pan over medium heat, add the orange juice, salt, pepper, and honey. Mix well; then add the parsnips, turning often and cooking until glazed. Add more butter and honey if the pan dries out.

Pastas

Baked Lasagne

Lasagne Noodles

Filling:
Choice of:
Spinach, washed and cooked
Ricotta, Mozzarella, Parmesan cheese
Tomato sauce, canned or homemade (see pages 70, 123)

Preheat oven to 350°F

First boil the strips or sheets of lasagne in a large saucepan with plenty of salted boiling water until tender. Arrange in a 9 x 12-inch baking dish, alternating layers of noodles with layers of filling. Pour the tomato sauce over the top and bake in the oven 10–20 minutes at 350°F until the filling is hot and the cheese is melted. The most delicious version of lasagne is to use all of the fillings between layers and to pour tomato sauce and cheese over the top.

Pasta al Pesto

Spaghetti or any other pasta, cooked
1 clove garlic
1 cup (1½ ounces) basil
1 tablespoon pine nuts (pignolias)
½ cup oregano
Good pinch cayenne pepper
½ cup olive oil
Salt and cayenne pepper
¼ cup Parmesan cheese, grated

Boil the pasta until tender in a large saucepan with plenty of salted, boiling water. As the pasta is cooking, make the pesto by grinding the herbs in a pestle or putting them in the blender. Then blend in the oil slowly until you have a smooth sauce that will pour easily. It should be a lovely green color. Add salt and cayenne pepper to taste, pour over the hot pasta and mix well; lifting it with care. Serve the grated cheese on the side.

Pasta and Peas with Sauce

3 tablespoons raw onion, minced
3 tablespoons olive oil
1 teaspoon dried thyme
1 teaspoon basil
Salt and pepper
2 pounds (2 cups hulled) green peas
2 tablespoons hot water
3 cups (12 ounces) spaghetti or macaroni
3 tablespoons butter

SAUCE:
3 cloves of garlic
2 tablespoons pignolias (pine nuts)
¼ cup Parmesan or Romano cheese
Olive oil
Salt and pepper
Grated cheese for the top

Sauté the onion for 5 minutes in a saucepan with the oil; add the herbs, seasonings, hulled peas and 2 tablespoons of hot water; simmer until tender. Boil the chosen pasta in a large saucepan for 10–12 minutes in salted water; then drain and mix in 3 tablespoons of butter.

To make the sauce: crush the garlic and mix with the nuts and cheese, purée in the blender with the oil, salt and pepper. Mix the peas and pasta, then stir in the sauce. Serve at once with a bowl of grated cheese on the side.

Noodles

¾ cup flour
Pinch of salt
1 egg yolk
A little water or milk

Mix the flour and salt in a bowl. Lightly beat the egg yolk and stir into the flour. Mix well and add a little milk or water if the paste is too stiff and will not bind. It will be a little sticky so knead it until it is smooth; then leave it in a cool place for ½ hour. Roll it out flat on a floured surface as thinly as possible; then roll it up into a long roll and cut into narrow ribbons with a very sharp knife. Let the noodles dry; then store them in an airtight can until needed. Cook them in boiling salted water until they are tender. These homemade noodles only take a few minutes to cook. Use with sauces or just grated cheese.

Green Peas and Cheese

2 pounds (2 cups hulled) green peas
¼ cup olive oil
1 clove garlic, crushed
4 green onions, minced
1 teaspoon honey
Salt and pepper
3 tablespoons water
1 teaspoon chervil
⅓ cup Parmesan cheese, grated

Hull the peas, then heat the olive oil in a thick saucepan; add the garlic and minced onion, and sauté over low heat for 8 minutes. Add the peas, honey, salt and pepper and 3 table-spoons of water. Cover and simmer over low heat until just tender, then add the crushed chervil. Serve sprinkled with cheese.

Fried Crispy Noodles

These morsels are delicious as a garnish with almost any savory dish.
Boil the noodles; do not let them get mushy. As the noodles are boiling, heat ¾-inch of oil in a deep frying pan. Drain the noodles well and drop them into the oil. Deep fry until crispy. Use a splatter cover to protect yourself from splattering hot oil. Drain on paper towels.

Pea Soufflé with Almonds

2 pounds (2 cups hulled) green peas
1 teaspoon butter
¼ cup water
2 tablespoons whole wheat flour
¼ cup toasted almonds, minced
½ cup cream
3 tablespoons milk
2 drops of almond or ratafia extract
3 eggs, separated
Salt and pepper

Preheat oven to 350°F

Hull and simmer the peas in a covered saucepan with the butter and ¼ cup of water. When tender, mash or purée the peas in a blender with the flour. There should be 2 cups of purée. Mix the almonds, cream, and milk together in a saucepan and bring just to the boiling point over medium-high heat. Add the pea purée and extract and beat in the egg yolks. Remove from the heat. Beat the egg whites to a stiff peak and fold into the first mixture, adding salt and pepper to taste. Pour into a greased soufflé dish and bake in the oven at 350°F for 30 minutes. Serve at once.

Peppers

The peppers given in the following recipes are the sweet green, red or yellow peppers, not the hot little chilies. Some dishes call for skinned peppers. Bake them in a hot oven until the skins blister, or even blacken a little, and then while they are still hot, put them into a paper bag or a steamer over hot water. Cover tightly and steam for a few minutes and the skins will come off quite easily. If peppers are being used for stuffing, boil them for 2–3 minutes, and then drain them. Always remove seeds and fibre.

Stuffed Baked Peppers

Select good-sized peppers. They may be stuffed whole but it is easier to cut them in halves to make cups or lengthwise to make boats. Remove the seeds and fibre and boil the peppers covered with water in a large saucepan for 3–4 minutes. Drain upside down and fill while still warm if they are to be baked, but if they are to be served cold, fill them when cold. Bake the peppers in the oven at 350°F for 15–18 minutes if they are filled with precooked stuffing, 25–30 minutes if they are filled with uncooked stuffing.

Jack Bean and Mushroom Stuffing

Mix equal quantities of precooked broad or "jack" beans, sautéed onion tops and chopped mushrooms. Fill the peppers and bake in the oven for 15 minutes at 350°F.

Italian Stuffing

Sauté some tiny bread cubes in olive oil with crushed garlic in a frying pan over medium heat; add a few sliced black olives. Stuff the peppers and bake in the oven for 30 minutes at 350°F. Tasty stuffing for both peppers and tomatoes.

There are many suitable stuffings, and leftover food is good served this way. Macaroni and cheese makes a good stuffing; mixed sweet corn and onions make a colorful stuffing...use your imagination!

Peppers, Tomatoes and Eggs

2 cups onions, finely diced
½ cup olive oil
4 large peppers, finely diced
Salt and pepper
1½ teaspoons oregano
Pinch of cumin
3 large ripe tomatoes, skinned and chopped
2 teaspoons honey
5 eggs, beaten

Preheat oven to 350°F

Cook the onions for 5 minutes in the olive oil in a large saucepan over medium heat; add the green peppers, and cook until just tender. Add the salt, pepper, oregano, cumin, tomatoes and honey. Cover and bake in the oven for ½ hour at 350°F or until very soft. If the sauce seems thin, uncover the dish or pan for the last 20 minutes to evaporate the liquid. When quite soft, add the beaten eggs and cook and stir on top of the stove over medium heat until the eggs are set. (They should be the consistency of scrambled eggs.) Serve without delay.

Baked Pumpkin

2 pounds pumpkin
8 tablespoons butter or margarine
4 tablespoons honey
3 ounces preserved ginger, chopped
Salt

Preheat oven to 350°F

Cut the pumpkin into serving pieces; de-seed and peel the wedges. Melt the butter in a small saucepan; stir in the honey and ginger. Score the pumpkin wedges with a knife and pour on the honey, butter and ginger mix. Sprinkle lightly with salt. Put the wedges in a 9 x 12-inch baking pan with ¼-inch of water in it and bake in the oven at 350°F for 1½ to 2 hours, basting often.

Baked Potatoes

Whenever it is possible, potatoes should be cooked in their skins. A medium-sized potato has the same number of calories as an orange and is a valuable part of our diet.

Baked potatoes are always popular and even little new potatoes may be cooked this way. Scrub the potatoes thoroughly; cover with plenty of water in a saucepan and boil just long enough to heat them through; then drain and bake in a hot oven. Old potatoes take from 40–60 minutes, starting at 375°F for 20 minutes and then 325°F for the rest of the time. Small new potatoes take half the time, baking at 375°F for 10 minutes and then 325°F for the rest of the time. Baked potatoes lend themselves to being stuffed. After they have been baked, split the skins along one side, scoop out most of the pulp, mix with the chosen ingredients, refill the skins and put them back in the oven at 250°F for 5–10 minutes to heat. Here are a few ideas for stuffing.

Stuffed Baked Potatoes

Leek Stuffing

Trim, wash and mince some leeks. Sauté them in a frying pan with butter, season with salt and pepper, stir in a dash of cream and then blend with the potato pulp.

Nut Stuffing

Mix some peanut butter or ground almonds with salt and pepper. Add some hot cream, a little margarine or butter and, if you like, a beaten egg. Blend well with the potato pulp.

Herb Stuffing

Mince some fresh parsley, basil, tarragon, chervil and chives, then blend with melted margarine, hot cream, salt, pepper, and potato pulp.

Cheese Stuffing

Blend 1 cup of grated cheddar cheese, 1 teaspoon thyme, hot cream, salt, pepper, melted butter, and potato pulp. After stuffing, sprinkle the tops of the potatoes with chopped parsley.

Mushroom Stuffing

Sauté chopped mushrooms in a frying pan with butter, chives, hot cream, tarragon and sherry. Blend into the potato pulp.

I hope this gives you some ideas, but they by no means exhaust the materials!

Potato and Almond Soufflé

2½ cups (5 medium) mashed potatoes
Dash of mace
Salt and pepper
½ cup Half and Half
4 eggs, separated
½ cup ground almonds

Preheat oven to 375°F

Boil the potatoes in their skins in a large saucepan with plenty of water. Skin and mash them to make 2½ cups of mashed potatoes. Mix together in a bowl all the ingredients, except the egg whites and ground almonds. Beat the egg whites to the stiff peak stage, then fold into the first mixture. Pour into a greased soufflé dish, sprinkle ground almonds on top, and bake in the oven for 20 minutes at 375°F. Other ingredients may be substituted for the same amount of potatoes, such as mashed turnip, rutabagas or carrots. A few peas add color.

Potato Pie

PASTRY SHELL:
1⅓ cups whole wheat flour
½ teaspoon salt
1 teaspoon baking powder
10 tablespoons butter
Milk to mix
2 tablespoons soft margarine

FILLING:
2¼ cups (4–5) potatoes, mashed
Salt and pepper
1 cup small curd cottage cheese
¼ cup sour cream
1 small onion, grated
1 egg, beaten

Preheat oven to 400°F

Make the pastry shell first by sifting the dry ingredients together in a bowl. Cut in the butter and enough milk to make a soft but not sticky dough. Roll it out on a floured surface and dot with the 2 tablespoons of soft margarine, fold over, roll out again and line an 8-inch pie pan with it.

To prepare the filling, boil the potatoes in their skins in a saucepan with plenty of water. Skin and mash them and blend with all the ingredients in the filling list. Fill the pastry shell with this and bake in the oven for 10 minutes at 400°F, then turn the heat down to 325°F and bake for another 20 minutes. Serve with poached eggs and tomato sauce.

Potatoes Chantilly

4 large white potatoes
1 cup whipped cream
Salt and cayenne pepper
Pinch of nutmeg
½ cup Parmesan cheese, grated

Preheat oven to 375°F

Boil the potatoes in a saucepan with plenty of water. Skin and dice the potatoes and place in a greased ovenware dish. Whip the cream to make 1 cup of whipped cream, season with salt, pepper and nutmeg, and spread on top of the potatoes. Sprinkle cheese on top and bake in the oven at 375°F for 7–8 minutes.

Rose Turnips

2½ cups (3–4) baby turnips
2½ tablespoons paprika
4 tablespoons sweet white wine
Salt and cayenne pepper
3 tablespoons margarine or butter
½ cup sour cream

Preheat oven to 350°F

Peel and slice the turnips into a greased casserole dish. Mix 1½ tablespoons of paprika with the wine and pour over the turnips. Sprinkle with cayenne pepper and salt, and dot with margarine. Cover and bake in the oven at 350°F for 20–30 minutes, or until the turnips are tender but not mushy. There should not be more than ¼ cup of liquid left in the casserole. Mix the remaining tablespoon of paprika into the sour cream, pour over the turnips, and serve hot.

Ratatouille

2 onions, sliced from the top down, not ringed
1 small eggplant, peeled and chopped
1½ cups olive oil
1 small zucchini, unpeeled and thickly sliced
1 cucumber, 4 inches long, peeled and thinly sliced
2 medium tomatoes, diced
3 sweet red peppers, de-seeded and cut into strips
¼ pound green beans
1 clove garlic, chopped
⅛ cup parsley, chopped
Good pinch of basil and thyme
1 bay leaf
8 peppercorns

Preheat oven to 350°F

Sauté the onions and eggplant in a large frying pan with half of the oil. When soft place them in a casserole with a tight lid, add the rest of the ingredients and bake at 350°F until the vegetables are tender (about 30 minutes). If the mixture looks too juicy remove the lid for the last 10 minutes of cooking time. Serve with Parmesan cheese and garlic-buttered toast.

Rice

Curried Rice Soufflé

1 cup dry white wine
1 cup Swiss cheese, grated
1 teaspoon prepared mustard
Pinch of cayenne pepper
½ teaspoon salt
2 teaspoons butter
1 teaspoon onion, grated
3 egg yolks, lightly beaten
3 egg whites
½ cup rice, precooked
1½ teaspoons curry powder
6 large individual soufflé dishes

Preheat oven to 400°F

If you do not have precooked rice on hand, add ¼ cup rice to ¾ cup boiling water in a saucepan, cover and simmer for 30–40 minutes until tender.

Heat the wine in a large saucepan, but do not boil it. Remove the pan from the heat and add the cheese, mustard, pepper, salt, butter, and onion. Stir until the cheese is partially melted, then pour the mixture over the lightly beaten egg yolks. Mix the cooked rice and curry powder together and stir into the first mixture. Season to taste. Beat the egg whites to the stiff peak stage and fold into the rice. Fill the soufflé dishes only three quarters full. Bake in the oven at 400°F for 20 minutes or until the soufflés are puffed and golden brown. Serve without delay.

California Rice and Olives

2 tablespoons olive oil
2 tablespoons butter
1¼ cups rice, uncooked
2 cloves garlic
4½ cups tomato juice
¾ cup sliced black olives
2 teaspoons chili powder
2 teaspoons salt
1 teaspoon dried dill

Preheat oven to 350°F

Heat the oil and butter together in a large frying pan over medium heat; brown the rice and crushed garlic in it. Lift out the garlic and add the tomato juice, olives, chili powder, salt, and dill. Pour into a greased baking dish and bake covered for 1 hour at 350°F, or until the rice is tender and all the moisture has been absorbed.

Pilaf

Each kind of Pilaf is made a little differently. The rice is fried in hot oil, then liquid is added, and the rice finishes cooking in the oven. It is important to use the right type of rice, as different rice types absorb different amounts of water. Use stock as liquid whenever possible. One cup of raw rice will, on the average, make 3 cups of cooked rice.

Eastern Rice

3 tablespoons margarine or olive oil
20–30 almonds, blanched
1 clove garlic, minced
1 onion, minced
3 cups long grain rice, uncooked
4½ cups vegetable stock (or water)
10 whole peppercorns
2 bay leaves
Salt
1 onion, cut in rings
¼ teaspoon saffron
Oil for frying
Flour
2 eggs, hard-boiled

Preheat oven to 350°F

Heat the olive oil in a large thick frying pan, add the almonds and fry over medium heat, stirring, until they begin to brown. Add the minced garlic and onion and sauté until the onion is transparent. Add the rice and stir-fry over medium heat until the rice is brown. Transfer to a large casserole; add the stock, peppercorns, bay leaves, salt, and saffron. Do not stir. Place on high heat and bring to a boil; cover and transfer to the oven. Bake for 20 minutes at 350°F. Heat 1 inch of oil in the bottom of a thick frying pan. Dip the onion rings in flour and fry in the hot oil until brown and crisp. Pile the rice high on a hot dish and garnish with slices of hard-boiled eggs and onion rings. A curry sauce may be served with this dish; however the dish is excellent as is.

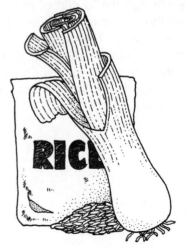

Tuscan Rice

1 cup rice, uncooked
3 egg yolks, beaten
1 tablespoon lemon juice
Pinch of cayenne pepper
⅔ cup Parmesan cheese, grated
3 tablespoons margarine
Lemon slices

Boil the rice in a large saucepan with 2 cups of salted water for 40–50 minutes or until tender, but not mushy. Drain the rice into a colander, but keep ½ cup of the water. Wash the rice well under running water to rinse off the excess starch and place in a large serving dish. Beat the egg yolks, lemon juice, and pepper into the ½ cup of rice water. Pour over the rice, mix in half the cheese and all the margarine. Mix well and serve with the rest of the cheese and small slices of lemon on the side. Rice cooked this way makes a good foundation for creamed eggs or root vegetables.

Orange and Thyme Rice

2 tablespoons butter
2 small onions, chopped
1 cup orange juice
1 cup water
1 tablespoon orange rind, grated
½ teaspoon salt
½ teaspoon dried thyme
1 cup brown rice, uncooked

Melt the butter in a frying pan over low heat, add the onion, and sauté until it is soft; add the orange juice, water, orange rind, salt, and thyme. Turn the heat up to high to bring to a boil; then add the rice slowly. Stir for a second or two; then cover the pan. Reduce the heat to low and simmer for 25–30 minutes until the rice is tender but firm.

Jamaica Rice and Beans

1¼ cups dried beans, your choice
4 cups cold water
⅔ cup desiccated coconut
1 large onion, diced
Oil for frying
2 cloves of garlic, crushed
1 teaspoon Worcestershire sauce
1 tablespoon dried herbs, mixed (your choice)
1 tablespoon honey
2 cups brown rice, uncooked
Salt and pepper

Wash the beans and soak them in a large covered saucepan with 4 cups of cold water for not less than 12 hours, more if possible. Then simmer them in the same water for 2 hours or until they are tender. Drain, pouring the water on top of the coconut. Leave the coconut to stand for 5 minutes to infuse; then strain, squeezing out all the liquid into a bowl. Discard the coconut. There should be 2½ cups of liquid; if less, add water.
Fry the onion in a little hot oil in a deep saucepan until slightly brown; then add all the other ingredients, including the rice and beans. Pour the coconut water over all, cover tightly, and cook over very low heat for 45 minutes. It should be a little damp. These amounts will serve a lot of people but it is just as good the next day, served as leftovers!

Spinach Cheese Balls

½ cup raw spinach, minced
½ cup cottage cheese
Salt and pepper
Pinch of nutmeg
1½ teaspoons orange peel, grated
1 large egg
2 tablespoons flour (approximately)
Cheese (your choice), grated
Salted water
Melted butter or margarine

Wash the spinach at least twice, mince, and press in a strainer to drain off the excess juice. Blend the cottage cheese in the blender until quite smooth; then mix with the spinach in a bowl and add the seasonings, orange rind, egg, flour, and 1 tablespoon of grated cheese. Add as little flour as possible to make the mixture bind. Mix well and roll into 20 balls. Boil the balls in a saucepan of boiling, salted water for not more than 3 minutes. Lift out with a slotted spoon. Pour melted butter over top and serve with grated cheese.

Spinach Roulade

1 cup raw spinach, minced

SAUCE:
3 tablespoons butter
1 tablespoon whole wheat flour
1 cup milk
Salt and pepper
3 eggs, separated
Bread crumbs

FILLING:
½ pound fresh mushrooms
2 tablespoons butter
1 cup sour cream

TOPPING:
3 tablespoons melted margarine
Parmesan cheese

Preheat oven to 375°F

Wash the spinach at least twice and mince. Pack it firmly into a cup and squeeze out the excess water.

Melt the butter in a saucepan, stir in the flour and milk, and cook over low heat until it thickens. Cook and stir for 3 more minutes, then add the salt, pepper, and beaten egg yolks. Mix in the spinach and fold in the stiffly beaten egg whites. Put a piece of waxed paper in a 12 x 16-inch baking pan with low sides and sprinkle with bread crumbs. Pour on the spinach mixture and bake in the oven at 375°F for 15–20 minutes.

Slice and sauté the mushrooms with 2 tablespoons of butter in a frying pan. Mix with the sour cream and spread over the baked spinach mixture. Roll the whole thing up into a roll, lifting the wax paper to help it. Do not try to roll it up without the paper and do not roll the wax paper inside of the roll. Put the roll on a hot plate, pour melted margarine over it, sprinkle with cheese, and serve at once.

Spinach in Madeira and Cream

3 pounds (3–4 bunches) spinach
4 tablespoons Madeira
2 cups cream
Salt and pepper

Wash the spinach at least twice, and steam for 10 minutes in a covered saucepan with only the water that clings to the leaves. Drain all the liquid from the pan and cook the spinach uncovered over low heat to evaporate the rest of the water. Be careful not to burn it at this stage! There should be no water left in the pan. Remove from the heat and add the Madeira. Heat, but do not boil, the cream in a small saucepan over medium heat until it is reduced by half. Stir it into the spinach, season with salt and pepper and serve at once. This is an extravagant recipe, but a cheaper version may be made if a smooth, rich white sauce (page 121) is used instead of the cream. Beat a raw egg into the sauce at the last minute.

Spinach Pie au Gratin

1 precooked pie shell (page 44)
2½ cups spinach, cooked, cold and chopped
½ cup cream
2 tablespoons soft butter or margarine
½ cup Gouda cheese, diced
Salt and pepper
¼ pound Gouda cheese, sliced

Preheat oven to 400°F

Make the pie shell first, bake, and set aside. Steam 2–3 bundles of well-washed spinach in a covered saucepan with 1 cup of water over medium heat. When tender, drain, chop, and refrigerate until cold. Mix the spinach, cream, butter, and diced cheese; season with salt and pepper and pour into the baked pie shell. Cover with sliced Gouda cheese and bake in the oven at 400°F until the cheese melts.

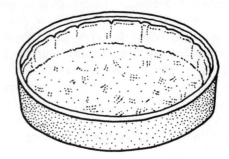

Martinique Yellow Squash

"Bouquet garni": 1 bay leaf, 6 sprigs parsley
1¾ pounds yellow squash (Hubbard, summer crookneck, etc.)
1 medium onion, minced
1 cup rich white sauce (page 121)
2 egg yolks, beaten
2 tablespoons grated Swiss cheese
Salt and cayenne pepper
Buttered bread crumbs

Preheat oven to 300°F

Make the "bouquet garni" by placing the bay leaf and parsley inside a piece of cotton material and tying it securely shut; or use a cotton tea bag.

Wipe and cut the squash into pieces. Put into a covered saucepan with just enough boiling water to prevent the squash from sticking to the bottom of the pan. Add the minced onion and the "bouquet garni"; cover and boil for 15 minutes over high heat. Drain; discard the bouquet. Make the white sauce, beat in the egg yolks and cheese; season with salt and cayenne pepper. Mix with the squash and put into a baking dish. Cover with some more cheese mixed with an equal quantity of buttered bread crumbs. Bake in the oven at 300°F for 35 minutes. Serve at once.

Baked Squash with Orange

4 cups (1 to 1½ pounds) yellow squash
1 tablespoon orange rind, grated
½ cup orange juice
2 tablespoons cream
1½ tablespoons butter
1 tablespoon honey
Salt and pepper
Pinch ground ginger

Preheat oven to 350°F

Peel and cut the squash into 2-inch cubes, place in an ovenware dish and bake in the oven at 350°F for 15 minutes. Remove from the heat, mash, and set aside. Mix all the other ingredients together in a large saucepan. Place over medium heat and bring to just below the boiling point; then mix in the squash. The mixture should be the consistency of fluffy mashed potatoes. Eat when hot, or, when cold make into small pancakes and fry.

Fried Squash with Caramel Sauce

2 crookneck squash
2 tablespoons light golden syrup or corn syrup
Cooking oil and butter for frying
Salt and pepper
¼ cup cream
Grated cheese for garnish

Do not peel the squash unless the skin seems coarse; just scrape and uncover the pale green skin that is underneath. If it is a really young squash, do not scrape or de-seed. Slice the squash into ¾-inch thick slices, de-seed. Mix the syrup with the oil and butter in a frying pan; add the squash and glaze the slices in the syrup-butter until almost burnt. Pepper and salt the slices, reduce the heat to low, and fry uncovered until just tender. This will take 8–10 minutes.

Place on a serving dish and keep warm in the oven at 200°F. Heat the cream to a boil in the squash frying pan, then reduce the heat to low and stir often until all the residue from the squash and syrup has dissolved into the cream. The cream will turn a rich brown. Pour the cream over the squash and top with cheese. The cheese may be omitted and corn flake crumbs used instead. Serve at once.

Squash Corn Bread

¾ cup (¼ to ½ pound) yellow squash
1 tablespoon baking soda
1 tablespoon cold water
1 tablespoon butter, melted
1 cup buttermilk
1 cup sour cream
1 tablespoon honey
2¼ cups cornmeal
1 teaspoon salt
2 eggs, separated

Preheat oven to 350°F

Wipe and cut the squash into pieces, and boil in a covered saucepan with just enough water to cover the squash. Cook over high heat until tender. Drain and mash. Use ¾ cup of the mashed squash for this recipe. Mix the baking soda with a tablespoon of cold water in a large bowl. Add all the other ingredients, except the egg whites. Beat the egg whites to the stiff peak stage and fold into the first mixture. Pour into a greased bread pan, and bake in the oven for ½ hour at 350°F. Slice and serve hot with butter or margarine.

Tomato Soufflé

1½ tablespoons butter or margarine
1 tablespoon mild onion, grated
1 cup tomato purée
Salt and pepper
Rind of 1 orange, grated
1 cup orange juice
½ cup whole wheat flour
4 eggs, separated

Preheat oven to 350°F

Melt the butter in a large frying pan over low heat. Sauté the grated onion until tender, then add the purée, salt, pepper, and orange rind and cook gently over low heat for 5 minutes. Mix the orange juice with the flour in a large bowl, add the beaten egg yolks, and mix well. Beat the egg whites until stiff and fold into the first mixture. Pour into a soufflé dish and bake in the oven for 25 minutes at 350°F.

Creole Tomatoes

6 very large, ripe tomatoes
1 large green pepper, minced
4 green onions, minced
Sea salt and pepper
Flour
2 tablespoons butter
½ cup dark molasses

Preheat oven to 300°F

Skin and slice the tomatoes into ½-inch slices crosswise. Place alternating layers of tomatoes, green pepper, and onion in a greased casserole dish. Sprinkle salt, pepper, and a little flour on each layer; dot with butter. Pour the molasses over the top and bake in the oven at 300°F for 1 hour.

Curried Tomatoes with Herbs

1 large tomato per person
Salt and pepper
Dried fennel, tarragon, basil, rosemary,
  summer savory, thyme

CURRY SAUCE:
1 tablespoon curry powder
1½ tablespoons oil or butter
2 tablespoons onion, grated
2½ teaspoons arrowroot or cornstarch
1 cup orange juice
1 teaspoon orange rind, grated
1 teaspoon honey
2 tablespoons sour cream (optional)

Preheat oven to 450°F

Skin and cut the tomatoes into crosswise slices, place in a greased baking dish, and sprinkle with salt, pepper, and all or some of the herbs.

Stir and cook the curry powder and butter together in the top of a double boiler over boiling water for 8 minutes. Add the onion and cook for 3 more minutes. Blend the arrowroot with the orange juice in a bowl, add to the onion mix, and stir in the rest of the ingredients. Cook over low heat in the double boiler until thickened. Add 2 tablespoons of sour cream, if you like. Bake the dish of tomatoes in the oven for 7–8 minutes at 400°F. Remove from the oven and cover with the sauce. Garnish to taste.

Green Tomatoes in Sour Cream

6 large green tomatoes, just tinged with red
2 tablespoons honey
½ cup tomato juice
Salt and pepper
½ cup sour cream

Do not try to use the tiny green tomatoes for this; they won't work! Cut each tomato in half crosswise, place in a saucepan, dot with honey, and add the tomato juice, salt and pepper. Simmer for 40 minutes over low heat to evaporate some of the juice. Heat the sour cream in a small saucepan over low heat, but do not boil or it will curdle. Pour over the tomatoes, and serve hot!

Tomato Pie Nicoise

Pastry shell and top (page 44)

6 tablespoons buttered bread crumbs
Some firm green or red tomatoes
Salt
Black pepper
3 tablespoons parsley, chopped
3 tablespoons chives, chopped
1 tablespoon olive oil
1 clove of garlic, minced
1 onion, cut in rings
1 cup (1 pound unshelled) green peas
12 black olives
1 tablespoon butter

Preheat oven to 450°F

Make the pastry first and line a pie pan with half the pastry. Cover with a layer of the bread crumbs, then put a layer of very thinly sliced tomatoes; sprinkle with salt, black pepper, parsley, chives, oil, and garlic. Add the rings of onion and peas. Place the rest of the slices of tomatoes on top, sprinkle with black pepper and some oil, and cover with a layer of sliced black olives. Dot with butter. Cover with a pastry top, flatten the rim, and trim neatly to seal it. Cut a few slashes in the top and bake in the oven at 450°F for 10 minutes, then lower the heat to 375°F and bake for 20 more minutes until the pastry is a delicate brown.

A nice additional touch is to pour 2 tablespoons of tomato juice mixed with 2 tablespoons of sherry into the slashes of the pastry top.

Stuffed Tomatoes

Large fresh tomatoes
Browned bread crumbs, mixed with
  melted butter
1 egg for each tomato
Cream
Grated cheese
Salt and pepper

Preheat oven to 350°F

Skin the tomatoes whole, slice ¼-inch off the tops and scoop out most of the insides. Put 1 tablespoon of bread crumbs in each tomato, drop in a raw egg, a little cream, and fill with grated cheese. Sprinkle with salt and pepper, place close together in a greased baking dish, and bake in the oven at 350°F for 15–20 minutes. If the tomatoes are very ripe do not skin them or they will burst.

Tomato Dumplings

Pastry dough (page 44)

6 ripe tomatoes
4 tablespoons honey
Salt and pepper
Milk

Preheat oven to 400°F

Make any of the pastry doughs on page 44 . Roll out and cut into 6 round shapes, each one large enough to enclose a tomato. Skin the tomatoes, cut a small hole on the top, and put a little honey, pepper and salt in each one. Sprinkle a little of the same mixture on each piece of pastry, dampen the edges, place a tomato in the center of each round, and bring the pastry up to cover the tomatoes. Seal carefully. Place the dumplings, seam side down, on a greased baking dish. Brush each one with a little milk and bake in the oven at 400°F for 30 minutes.

Baked Tomatoes Stuffed with Rice

6 medium tomatoes
1 cup cooked brown rice, lightly seasoned
  with curry powder
3 teaspoons onion, grated
Buttered bread crumbs

Preheat oven to 400°F

If you do not have any precooked brown rice on hand, add ⅓ cup raw rice to 1 cup of salted, boiling water. Cover and simmer for 30–45 minutes until tender. Season lightly with curry powder and set aside. Cut a thin slice from the stem ends of the tomatoes; scoop out the pulp and mix it with the flavored rice and grated onion. Stuff the tomatoes with the mixture, place on a greased baking dish, sprinkle with buttered bread crumbs, and bake in the oven at 400°F for 25–30 minutes.

These tomatoes are delicious served on a bed of chopped, steamed spinach.

Indian Vegetable Curry

SAUCE:
4 tablespoons vegetable oil
2 cloves of garlic, crushed
1 very large onion, grated

1 tablespoon turmeric
1 tablespoon coriander
1 teaspoon cardamom, crushed
1 teaspoon ground ginger
¼ teaspoon chili powder
1 teaspoon cumin powder
1 teaspoon caraway powder
½ teaspoon ground cloves

3 tablespoons currants
½ teaspoon dry mustard
1 tablespoon honey
3 tablespoons chutney
Salt
½ cup desiccated coconut
1 cup vegetable stock or water
½ cup tomato juice
2 tablespoons lemon or lime juice

COOKED VEGETABLES:
Steamed cauliflower
Broiled tomatoes
Steamed parsnips
Steamed little onions
Hot boiled rice and Indian chutney

Heat the oil in the top of a double boiler, add the garlic, onions, and all the dry ingredients; cook over simmering water for 10 minutes, then add the rest of the sauce ingredients. Stir well, cover, and leave to cook at the same heat for 45 minutes. If the list of ingredients seems intimidating, you may use 3 tablespoons of commercial curry powder, but it is more satisfying to make your own.

Always use long grain rice. Add 1 part raw rice to 2 parts boiling water, cover, and simmer for 40–55 minutes until tender, drain and rinse well.

Cook your choice of vegetables, place on a hot serving dish, and pour the sauce over them. This is not an excessively strong curry sauce, and real addicts may want to add red pepper. Almost any vegetables may be used, either together or separately.

Serve with the rice, a little dish of nuts, plenty of sweet mango chutney, and a small bowl of grated coconut.

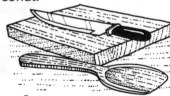

Baked Vegetables Mixed with Rice

1 cup brown rice, uncooked
½ cup carrots, diced
½ cup turnips, diced
½ cup cabbage, shredded
2 potatoes, peeled and thinly sliced
1 onion, peeled and thinly sliced
1 cup tomatoes, diced
½ teaspoon parsley, chopped
½ teaspoon dried basil
Salt and pepper
4 cups strong vegetable stock

Preheat oven to 325°F

Put the rice, carrots, turnips, and cabbage into a greased baking dish. Layer with potatoes, then onions, then tomatoes. Season with the herbs, salt and pepper. Pour the stock on top, cover, and bake in the oven for 3 hours at 325°F, or until the vegetables are tender and the rice is cooked.

Zucchini Provencale

2 pounds (6 medium-sized) zucchini
1 medium onion, sliced
4 tablespoons vegetable oil
4 large tomatoes, peeled and quartered
1 green pepper, de-seeded and finely chopped
1 clove garlic, crushed
Salt and pepper
Garnish of chopped parsley mixed with
*   Parmesan cheese*

Wash, peel, and cut the zucchini into cubes. Sauté the onion in a frying pan with the oil over low heat for 5 minutes; add the tomatoes, green pepper, and crushed garlic. Season with salt and pepper, and cook for 15 minutes over low heat. Lift out the garlic, add the zucchini; cover and cook over low heat until the zucchini is tender. Put on a hot serving dish and garnish with parsley and cheese.

Vegetable Stew with Pinwheel Top

1 cup (1 pound unshelled) green peas, steamed
1 cup green beans, steamed and chopped
3 carrots, boiled and sliced
1 cup tomatoes, steamed and sliced
16 cocktail onions, boiled
2 cups milk
1 bay leaf
2 cloves
2 tablespoons butter or margarine
4 tablespoons whole wheat flour
Salt and pepper
1 teaspoon curry powder
1 teaspoon milk

PINWHEEL TOP:
1½ cups whole wheat flour
3 teaspoons baking powder
½ teaspoon celery salt
4 tablespoons butter
1 cup sharp cheese, grated
Cold vegetable stock or water

Preheat oven to 425°F

Pinwheel top: Sift the flour, baking powder, and celery salt into a mixing bowl; cut in the butter until finely blended, then add the grated cheese. Moisten with enough cold vegetable stock to make a soft dough. Roll the dough out on a floured surface to ¼-inch thick, sprinkle with more cheese and roll up into a 1-inch diameter roll. Place the roll in the refrigerator until it is needed. Cut into thin slices and arrange close together on top of the dish of vegetables.

Vegetable stew: Precook the vegetables separately in as little water as possible. Scald the milk in a small saucepan with the bay leaf and cloves. In a separate saucepan, melt the butter over low heat, and blend in 4 tablespoons of flour. Cook and stir over low heat until it bubbles, then add the scalded milk; continue to cook until thick and smooth. Season with salt and pepper, and a paste of curry powder mixed with a little cold milk. Bring to a boil over high heat and cook for 5 minutes. Stir in the vegetables and pour into a large casserole dish. Remove the dough from the refrigerator, cut into thin slices and arrange the pinwheel shapes close together on top of the vegetables. Bake in the oven at 425°F for 20 minutes. Serve at once.

Sauces

Basic Quick White Sauce

2 tablespoons butter
2 tablespoons flour
1 cup milk
Salt and pepper

Melt the butter in a saucepan over low heat, slowly stir in the flour, and cook for 5 minutes, stirring continuously. Gradually stir in the milk and season to taste. Stir and cook until it thickens into a creamy consistency. You can thicken white sauce by cooking it longer, or adding a little more flour. You can thin it by not cooking it so long, or adding a little more milk.

Lemon Caper Sauce

½ cup vegetable liquid or water
2 tablespoons margarine
1 tablespoon onion, grated or
  1 tablespoon onion salt
Pepper and salt (do not add salt if using onion salt)
1 teaspoon turmeric
1 teaspoon arrowroot
2 tablespoons capers
Parsley as garnish

Blend the first five ingredients together in a saucepan. Blend in 1 teaspoon of arrowroot; cook and stir over low heat until it thickens. Add the capers, pour over the vegetable, and serve with parsley sprinkled on top.

Mushroom Sauce

1½ cups vegetable liquid or water
¼ cup cream
4 teaspoons arrowroot
3 tablespoons onion, chopped
Salt and cayenne pepper
Pinch nutmeg
½ pound (1 cup sautéed) mushrooms
4 teaspoons margarine
Parsley or chives as garnish

Blend the vegetable liquid with the cream and arrowroot in a saucepan. Add the other ingredients and cook over low heat, stirring, until it thickens. Pour over the chosen vegetable and garnish with chopped parsley or chives.

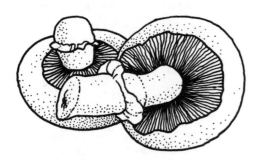

Mustard Sauce

4 tablespoons butter or margarine, melted
¼ teaspoon honey
1 teaspoon dry mustard
2 teaspoons lemon juice
Salt and pepper
Pinch of nutmeg

Mix all the ingredients in a saucepan and simmer over low heat to thicken. Beat with a whisk, or stir well, and pour over the vegetable main dish.

Nut Sauce

1 cup nuts, any mixture
1 teaspoon honey
2 teaspoons lemon juice
1½ cups mayonnaise

Preheat oven to 300°F

Bake the nuts on a cookie sheet in the oven at 300°F for 20 minutes. Remove from the oven and rub on a towel to rub off the skins. Grind or blend them to a fine consistency in the blender. Mix with the lemon juice and honey; fold in the mayonnaise last.

Tomato Sauce

3 tablespoons onion, chopped
3 tablespoons green pepper, chopped
¼ cup water
Tomato juice
3 teaspoons arrowroot
3 tablespoons sour cream
Bran as garnish

Boil the onions and green pepper in ¼ cup of water until just tender. Strain off the liquid and add enough tomato juice to make ¾ cup of liquid. Blend with the arrowroot in a saucepan and cook over low heat until it thickens. Remove from the heat and mix in the sour cream, green peppers, and onions. Pour over the main vegetable dish and sprinkle bran on top.

Chapter Four — Salads

Chapter Four — Salads

A collection of salad dressing and mayonnaise recipes are listed in the next chapter; some of them can make plain lettuce a gastronomic treat. Unless otherwise specified, the dressing is served separately.

Apple and Celery Salad

1 medium apple, diced
1 cup (3–4 stalks) celery hearts, diced
Salt and pepper
2 teaspoons pimiento, minced
1 teaspoon chives, minced
A little lemon juice
Mayonnaise (see page 174)

Peel, core, and dice the apple; cover the diced pieces with water and lemon juice in a bowl. In a separate bowl mix the remaining ingredients together; drain and add the apple; add enough mayonnaise to bind the salad together.

Stuffed Artichoke Salad

4 artichokes
Lemon juice
4 tomatoes
Mayonnaise
Salt and pepper
2 hard-boiled eggs
Watercress

Choose small, young and tender artichokes. Cut off the stalks and trim the leaves. Bring a little water and lemon juice to a boil, add the artichokes, cover and cook gently until tender, drain and leave to cool. Remove the inner leaves and center. Skin and chop the tomatoes and season with mayonnaise, salt and pepper; then fill the cavities of the artichokes with the tomato mix. Garnish to taste with the hard-boiled eggs and watercress.

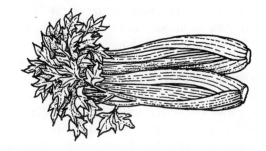

Artichoke Ring

5 eggs, hard-boiled and finely chopped
2 cups artichoke pulp
1 teaspoon powdered agar-agar or
  2 sticks of agar-agar
¼ cup cold water
1 level teaspoon salt
½ cup French dressing
½ cup chili sauce
½ cup mayonnaise
½ cup whipped cream
¼ teaspoon paprika
½ cup stuffed olives, thinly sliced

Boil 5 eggs in a small saucepan with plenty of water until hard boiled, 10–15 minutes. Drain, peel, and finely chop; set aside in a small bowl. Boil 3–4 globe artichokes until tender, approximately 30 minutes, in a covered saucepan with plenty of boiling, salted water. Drain well, scrape off the tender pulp from each leaf, and discard the rest of the leaf. Scrape away and discard the prickly "choke." Finely chop the remaining artichoke hearts and mix with the pulp. Soak the agar-agar in a bowl with ¼ cup of cold water for 5 minutes. Place in the top of a double boiler over boiling water and stir until dissolved. Stir in the salt, French dressing, chili sauce, mayonnaise, whipped cream, and paprika. When blended, stir in the artichoke pulp, chopped hard-boiled eggs, and sliced olives. Pour into a ring mold which has been rinsed in cold water or lightly oiled and refrigerate until firm. Serve on top of crisp lettuce. For a luxury salad, fill the center of the ring with chopped pimiento and whipped cream. For more ordinary occasions, fill the center with potato salad.

Ashville Salad

1 teaspoon agar-agar powder or
  1 stick agar-agar
½ cup cold water
1 large (17-ounce) can tomato soup
2 cups (1 pound) cream cheese
2 small green peppers, de-seeded and diced
2–3 stalks celery, chopped
Generous pinch of salt
Lettuce

Dissolve the agar-agar in a small bowl with ½ cup of cold water. Heat the soup in a saucepan over medium heat, add the agar-agar, cream cheese, green pepper, celery, and salt; mix well. Rinse six molds (custard cups) in cold water and pour the mixture into them. Chill in the refrigerator until firm then serve on a bed of lettuce. Serves six.

Avocado Mold

1 tablespoon agar-agar powder or
    1 stick agar-agar
3 tablespoons cold water
½ cup hot water
½ cup whipped cream
½ cup mayonnaise
2 cups mashed avocado
1 level teaspoon salt
1 teaspoon onion juice
Garnish of lettuce or tomato wedges
French dressing

Soak the agar-agar in a bowl with 3 table-spoons of cold water. Add the agar-agar to ½ cup boiling water in a bowl. Whip the whipping cream to the stiff peak stage, fold into the mayonnaise, then fold into the agar-agar mixture. Peel and de-seed several avocados and mash the pulp; use enough avocados to make 2 cups of pulp. Fold in the avocado pulp, salt, and onion juice. Rinse a ring mold form with cold water and pour in the mixture. Chill in the refrigerator until firm, turn out onto a dish, and serve garnished with lettuce or tomato wedges. Sprinkle the lettuce with French dressing to make it glossy. Serves six.

Avocado-Blue Cheese Salad

2 cups avocado, diced
1 cup celery, sliced
½ cup blue cheese, crumbled
1 cup mayonnaise
2 teaspoons lemon juice
Lettuce

Mix the first 5 ingredients together in a bowl in the order given. Serve on a bed of lettuce.

Autumn Salad

1 small firm green cabbage
1 mild onion, chopped
½ cup raisins
2 raw carrots, grated
1 cup cheddar cheese, diced

Discard the outside cabbage leaves, rinse the cabbage head under cold running water, and drain well. Shred the cabbage and mix all the ingredients together. Serves four.

Avocado Surprise

2 large avocados
6 tablespoons cottage cheese
2 tablespoons olives, minced
2 tablespoons chives, minced
2 tablespoons walnuts, chopped
Lettuce
French dressing

Cut the avocados in halves lengthwise, remove the pits, and peel off the skins very carefully so as not to mash the avocado. Mix the cheese, olives, chives, and nuts together in a bowl and fill the cavities of each avocado half with the mixture. Place the halves together to form a whole avocado again, with the stuffing in the middle; wrap in wax paper, and refrigerate for three hours. Serve whole or separate halves on a bed of lettuce, sprinkled with dressing. Serves two to four.

Bean Sprout and Tomato Salad

6 firm ripe tomatoes
Salt and pepper
1¼ pounds (2–3 cups) bean sprouts, chopped
2 teaspoons parsley or chervil
1 green pepper, de-seeded and chopped
3 stalks of celery, thinly sliced
Mayonnaise
Paprika
Lettuce

Scoop the centers of the tomatoes into a small bowl and cut a small slice off the bottom of each tomato so that they will stand upright. Drain and chill upside down in the refrigerator on a rack over a pan to catch the juice. Chop and season the pulp with salt and pepper, and press in a sieve over the sink to drain off any surplus liquid. Mix with the bean sprouts, parsley, green pepper, and celery; moisten with mayonnaise, and stuff the icy cold tomatoes. Sprinkle a dash of paprika on top of each tomato, and serve on a long dish lined with crisp lettuce leaves. Serves six.

Bean Sprouts and Watercress Salad

1 cup bean sprouts
¼ cup water chestnuts, sliced
½ cup pineapple chunks
¼ cup green pepper, slivered

1 cup mayonnaise
1 teaspoon soy sauce
1 teaspoon curry powder
Lettuce or watercress
Toasted almonds

Wash and drain the bean sprouts. Mix in a bowl with the water chestnuts, pineapple chunks, and green pepper. Mix the mayonnaise, soy sauce, and curry powder together in a separate bowl; blend well, then carefully stir into the sprouts mixture. Serve in individual bowls over a bed of lettuce or watercress, sprinkled with toasted almonds.

Bean Salad

2 cups cooked or canned (17-ounce) beans
   of your choice
Lettuce
4-inches of cucumber, peeled or scored, sliced
3 tomatoes, sliced
1 cup (1 pound unshelled) green peas, cooked
3 artichoke hearts
Few young spinach leaves, raw
French dressing

Place the beans in the center of a round flat serving dish on top of a bed of lettuce. Arrange the rest of the vegetables around the beans to create an attractive dish. Sprinkle with dressing just before serving. Serves four.

Fresh Beet Salad

2–3 small beets
Olive oil
Fresh lemon juice
Lettuce
Chopped parsley

Scrub, peel, and finely grate the beets. Mix in a bowl with a little oil and fresh lemon juice. Serve piled on top of a bed of lettuce leaves, garnished with parsley.

Beet Aspic

8 young beets
6 cloves
1½ cups warm water
4 teaspoons honey
Salt and pepper
1 teaspoon agar-agar powder or
   1 stick of agar-agar
Juice of 1 lemon, strained
Orange, lemon, or grapefruit juice, strained
½ cup white or red wine

Wash and grate the beets. Place in a saucepan with the cloves and 1½ cups of warm water; cover and simmer for 20 minutes over low heat. Strain and keep the liquid, but do not press the pulp as it will make the juice cloudy. Discard the beet pulp. Add the honey and seasonings to the beet juice. Soak the agar-agar in the lemon juice. Add enough fruit juice to the beet liquid to make five cups of liquid.

Heat the beet juice in a saucepan over medium heat, add the steeped agar-agar and stir until the agar-agar is melted. Remove from the heat and, when it is cool, add the wine. Pour into individual glass molds (custard cups), or put all of it into a ring mold. Refrigerate and chill until firm. Serve on a bed of lettuce with any preferred garnish.

Beet and Curry Powder Salad

½ cup vinegar or lemon juice
½ cup salad oil
1 teaspoon honey
Salt
½ teaspoon curry powder
1 medium (12-ounce) can beets,
   drained and diced
1 medium onion, diced
Lettuce

Mix the vinegar, oil, honey, salt, and curry powder together in a jar; shake well until mixed. Mix the beets and onion together in a bowl, add the dressing, and blend well. Refrigerate for several hours. Serve on a bed of lettuce.

Broccoli Salad

½ bunch (2–3 stalks) broccoli
1 small onion, chopped
1 teaspoon capers, minced
Salad dressing or mayonnaise
2 tomatoes

Break the broccoli into sprigs, boil in a saucepan with 1 cup of boiling, salted water for 10 minutes; drain and rinse in cold water. Place in a covered bowl and refrigerate for 20 minutes. Mix the chopped onion and capers in a bowl with some mayonnaise or dressing; pour over the chilled broccoli. Serve with tomato wedges as a garnish.

Red Cabbage Salad

1 red cabbage
2 tablespoons green pepper, chopped
3 tablespoons chives, minced
2 tablespoons celery, thinly sliced
2 tablespoons vegetarian sausage, sliced
  into ½-inch slices (optional)
French dressing

Shred the cabbage and mix with the rest of the ingredients in a salad bowl. Blend with French dressing.

Stuffed Cabbage Salad

1 medium green cabbage
1 medium red cabbage
Mayonnaise or salad dressing
1 clove of garlic, finely minced
Grated cheddar cheese

Discard the outside leaves of each cabbage. Wash and drain the cabbage heads, and level off the bases so that they will stand upright. Slice off the top of each cabbage and scoop out the centers with a sharp pointed knife. Shred the centers separately and mix with mayonnaise and finely minced garlic. Fill the cavity of the red cabbage with the white cabbage mixture and vice versa. Serve side by side on a generous bed of grated cheese.

Cheese and Carrot Salad

1 medium carrot
1 tablespoon French dressing
2 tablespoons grated cheese

Shred the carrot, blend with the dressing in a bowl. Either blend in the cheese with the carrot, or sprinkle it on top. Serve on lettuce. Makes one serving.

Cauliflower Salad

1 cauliflower
4 eggs
⅓ cup (⅓ pound unshelled) green peas
1 cup (¼ pound) lima beans
Oil for frying
1 zucchini
1 clove garlic, crushed
4 teaspoons capers
French dressing or mayonnaise
Chicory

Steam the cauliflower in a saucepan with ½ cup of water for 10–15 minutes. Drain and refrigerate until well-chilled. Boil 4 eggs in a saucepan with plenty of water until hard-boiled (10–15 minutes); drain, peel, and cut into quarters. Shell the peas and cook in ¼-inch of water in a saucepan over medium heat for 10 minutes; drain and chill. Boil the lima beans in a saucepan with 2 cups of salted water until tender (20–30 minutes); drain and chill. Heat a little oil in a frying pan, add the sliced zucchini and crushed garlic, and sauté until tender; chill.

When all the vegetables have been cooked and chilled, separate the cauliflower into little florets and mix in a bowl with the peas, lima beans, capers, zucchini, salad dressing, or mayonnaise. Serve on a bed of chicory, garnished with the hard-boiled egg. This is an excellent salad for a party because it is so easy to make.

Californian Salad

4-inches of cucumber
Lemon juice
3 tablespoons celery, chopped
2 dessert apples, cored and sliced
2 bananas
4 tomatoes
Salt
Mayonnaise or salad dressing
Lettuce

Wipe, but do not peel the cucumber; dice with the celery. Slice the apple and sprinkle with lemon juice. Thinly slice the bananas and tomatoes and sprinkle with salt. Gently mix all the ingredients together in a bowl with mayonnaise or salad dressing. Serve piled on a bed of shredded lettuce. Serves four.

Carrot and Onion Salad

¾ pound baby carrots
2 small onions or
   6 green onions
Parsley
Mayonnaise
Mustard leaves, watercress, or lettuce

Cook the carrots in a saucepan over medium-high heat in boiling, salted water until they are just tender but still crisp. Drain, let cool, and cut into slices. Cut the onions into thin rings and mix with the carrots. Chop a handful of parsley and mix with the mayonnaise. Blend all the ingredients together and serve on a bed of mustard leaves and watercress, or lettuce.

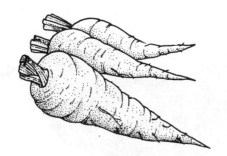

Carrot and Raisin Salad

½ cup seedless raisins
1 large raw carrot, shredded
1–2 stalks celery, finely sliced
½ cup walnuts
Salt
4 teaspoons mayonnaise
Lettuce or endive

Soak the raisins in a bowl for 15 minutes, covered with hot water; drain and let cool. Mix with the remaining ingredients in a bowl and chill well. Serve on lettuce or endive. Serves four.

Cheese Salad Bowl

1 medium potato
1¼ cup green cabbage, shredded
1 apple, cored and diced
2 tablespoons mixed pickles, chopped
½ cup cheddar cheese, diced
Salad dressing to taste
Lettuce or salad greens

Boil the potato in a saucepan with plenty of water until tender; drain, let cool, and cut into slices. Mix the ingredients together and gently blend in the dressing. Serve piled in a bowl on top of a bed of salad greens.

Cheese and Celery Salad

½ cup (4 ounces) cream cheese
2 tablespoons celery, chopped
2 tablespoons dessert apple, chopped
1 teaspoon parsley, minced
Celery sticks

Mix the cream cheese, chopped celery, apple, and parsley together in a bowl. Arrange on a dish over a bed of lettuce with several sticks of celery at each end. This makes a delicious hors d'oeuvre.

Cheese and Prune Salad

12 large prunes
½ cup (4 ounces) cream cheese
2 teaspoons chives, finely chopped
1 teaspoon parsley, chopped
1 teaspoon gherkin pickles, chopped
1 tablespoon mayonnaise

Lettuce
French dressing

Soak the prunes overnight in a bowl with cold tea or cold water. Mix the next five ingredients together. Remove the prune pits and fill the cavities with the cheese mixture. Toss the lettuce with the French dressing and arrange it in a bowl with the prunes on top.

Molded Cheese Salad

1 packet lemon Jell-o
2 cups boiling water
½ cup cream, whipped
1¼ cups nuts, chopped
½ cup sharp cheese, grated
1 can (8¾-ounce) crushed pineapple
½ cup stuffed olives, sliced
Cooked salad dressing (see page 170)

Dissolve the Jell-o in a bowl with 2 cups of boiling water and chill until it starts to set. Remove from the refrigerator and whip until it is light and fluffy. Fold in the next 5 ingredients. Pour into an oiled or rinsed ring mold and chill again until firm. Turn out and fill the center with the dressing.

Cheese and Tomato Crown

RED MOLD:
1 teaspoon powdered agar-agar or
⅔ stick agar-agar
1 large (17-ounce) can Italian tomatoes
¼ teaspoon salt
Dash of pepper
1 bay leaf
1 stalk celery, chopped
2 teaspoons vinegar or lemon juice
1 teaspoon onion juice

Soak the agar-agar in a bowl with ½ cup of cold water for 5 minutes. Cook the tomatoes for 10 minutes over low heat in a saucepan with the seasonings, bay leaf, and celery. Strain and keep the juice, discard the pulp. Add the agar-agar, vinegar or lemon juice, and onion juice to the juice. Stir until the agar-agar is dissolved. Pour into a fluted mold and chill until firm.

WHITE MOLD:
1 teaspoon agar-agar powder or
⅔ stick agar-agar
2 cups (1 pound) cottage cheese
Salt and paprika
½ cup milk

Soften the agar-agar for 5 minutes in a bowl with 4 tablespoons of cold water. Blend together in a bowl the cheese, salt, paprika, and milk. Place the agar-agar in the top of a double boiler and heat over hot water until dissolved, then add to the cheese mixture, and mix well. Pour into a fluted mold the same size as the red mold and chill until firm. Turn out both molds and cut each one into the same number of wedges. Arrange together as one mold, alternating the wedges. Serve garnished with watercress, lettuce, or endive.

Either of the above molds may be served separately.

Cream Cheese and Peanut Salad

1 large head of lettuce
½ cup (6 ounces) cream cheese
4 tablespoons French dressing
¾ cup peanuts, finely chopped

Set aside 4 large leaves of lettuce and tear up the rest. Mix the cheese, French dressing, and half the peanuts with the shredded lettuce. Line a salad bowl with the large lettuce leaves, put the mixture in the middle, and sprinkle the rest of the nuts on top. Serves six.

Swiss Cheese and Potato Salad

1 pound Swiss cheese
5 medium potatoes, boiled and chilled
1 small onion, minced
½ teaspoon salt
Dash of pepper
1 cup french dressing

Cut the cheese and precooked potatoes into small cubes and mix with the rest of the ingredients in a large bowl. Chill for one hour. Serve on or with any green salad. Serves eight.

Citrus Salad

1 large lettuce
A little watercress
1 grapefruit, sectioned and peeled
2 oranges, sectioned and peeled
12 dates, pitted
2 ounces preserved ginger, chopped
Citrus dressing (page 171)
6 tablespoons (3 ounces) cream cheese

Tear the lettuce and watercress into bite-size pieces, place in a salad bowl; add the grapefruit, oranges, dates, and ginger. Moisten lightly with citrus dressing and serve with cream cheese crumbled on top. Serves four.

Chicory Salad

6 tablespoons mayonnaise
4 tablespoons tomato sauce
3–4 tablespoons sour cream
1 tablespoon creamed horseradish
Chicory or endive

Mix the first four ingredients together in a salad bowl, add the chicory or endive and toss well. Serve chilled.

Coleslaw #1

½ small firm green cabbage
3 stalks celery
Mayonnaise or salad dressing

Wash and cut the cabbage into quarters. Thinly slice each quarter and place the slices in a bowl with ice cold water; refrigerate for 15 minutes. Drain and dry carefully. Blend in a bowl with the finely chopped celery and mayonnaise.

Variation: Add chopped apple, chopped nuts, or raisins for a tasty variation.

Coleslaw #2

1 small head green cabbage
1–2 teaspoons French mustard
1 cup mayonnaise
1 teaspoon honey
A little sliced onion or green pepper

Wash and shred only the heart of the cabbage, place in a bowl with ice cold water, and refrigerate for 15 minutes. Drain, dry carefully, and refrigerate. Stir together in a bowl the mustard, mayonnaise, and honey; then blend with the chilled cabbage. Pile on a serving dish and garnish with chopped onion or green pepper.

Coleslaw with Fruit

2 cups green cabbage, shredded
2 tablespoons honey
4 tablespoons sour cream
¼ cup green pepper, minced
Salt and pepper
Lemon juice
Powdered fennel (optional)

Choice of: Seedless grapes, cantaloupe or
    melon balls, sliced fresh peaches,
    pitted cherries, or sour apple slices.

Soak 2 cups of shredded cabbage in a bowl with cold water for 15 minutes; drain, and refrigerate. Assemble this salad just before serving or else it becomes soggy. Toss the chosen fruit with the cabbage, dribble honey over top, and add the rest of the ingredients.

Variations: For a richer dressing add more sour cream. Substitute powdered anise for the powdered fennel to create a delightful and unusual flavor.

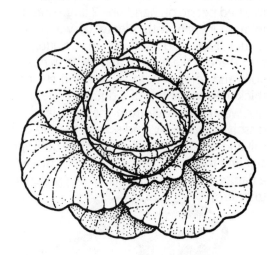

Coral Salad

¾ teaspoon agar-agar powder or
  ⅔ stick agar-agar
3 tablespoons cold water
1½ cups creamy mashed potato
1 egg, separated
1 cup tomato pulp, strained
Salt and pepper to taste

Soak the agar-agar in a bowl with 3 table-spoons of cold water. If you do not have any mashed potato on hand boil 2 large potatoes in a saucepan with plenty of water until tender. Drain and mash with milk, butter, and salt. Place in the blender and blend in the egg yolk and tomato pulp. Cook and stir until thickened in the top of a double boiler over hot water. Remove from the heat, add the dissolved agar-agar, and season to taste with salt and pepper. Beat the egg white until very stiff and fold into the first mixture. Turn into a dampened mold and chill in the refrigerator until firm.

Cranberry Ring

1 pound cranberries
1¼ cups cold water
7 tablespoons honey
¾ teaspoon agar-agar or
  1 stick agar-agar
3 tablespoons water
½ cup nuts, chopped
3 stalks celery, chopped
Lettuce
Mayonnaise

Boil the cranberries in a saucepan with 1¼ cups water until the skins pop. Add the honey and cook gently over low heat for 5 minutes. Soak the agar-agar in 3 tablespoons of water and add to the cranberries. Chill until it starts to thicken, remove from the refrigerator, and fold in the nuts and celery. Pour into a ring mold and chill again until firm. Serve on a bed of lettuce leaves, topped with mayonnaise.

Variation: Serve with the center of the mold filled with potato salad or pimiento chopped in whipped cream. A really magnificent effect may be had if the cranberry ring is further garnished with pineapple slices propped against the sides. Fill the pineapple hole with stiff mayonnaise and top with a cherry on a toothpick.

Cucumber and Apricot Salad

2 cucumbers
1 teaspoon salt
4 tablespoons syrup from canned apricots
½ teaspoon fresh tarragon or
  1 teaspoon dried tarragon
2 tablespoons apple cider vinegar
1 teaspoon honey
Dash of pepper
Salad greens

Peel and slice the cucumbers into paper thin slices. Place in a salad bowl, sprinkle with salt, and cover with a plate with a weight on top of it. Leave to stand at room temperature for 6–8 hours; drain off the water at regular intervals. Mix the apricot syrup, tarragon, vinegar, and honey together in a bowl. Season with pepper and add more vinegar if the dressing is too sweet for your taste.

Pour the dressing over the cucumbers, mix lightly, cover, and refrigerate for 1 hour. Serve in a chilled bowl lined with crisp lettuce leaves.

Molded Cucumber Salad

1 small cucumber
½ pimiento
¼ teaspoon salt
½ teaspoon lemon juice
¾ teaspoon powdered agar-agar or
  ⅔ stick agar-agar
1 cup cold water
1 cup whipping cream
Salad greens

Peel the cucumber and dice together with the pimiento. Mix the cucumber, salt, pimiento, and lemon juice together in a bowl. Soak the agar-agar in 1 cup cold water for 5 minutes, then dissolve it in the top of a double boiler over hot water. Whip the whipping cream to the stiff peak stage, blend in the dissolved agar-agar, and fold into the first mixture. Pour into individual molds or custard cups and chill until set. Serve with lettuce, chicory, or endive. Serves four.

Dandelion Salad

4-6 ounces dandelion leaves, young leaves only
2 hard-boiled egg yolks
1 level teaspoon French mustard
Salt, pepper, paprika
1 tablespoon garlic or tarragon vinegar
3 tablespoons olive or salad oil

Use only young dandelion leaves picked when the flowers are just in bud in the spring; trim, wash, and dry them. If you do not have hard-boiled eggs on hand, boil two eggs in a saucepan with plenty of water for 8–12 minutes. Drain, peel and let cool. Mash the egg yolks, add the rest of the ingredients in the order given, and blend well. Add the dandelion leaves just before serving and toss lightly.

Dandelion and Orange Salad

Dandelion leaves
Orange peel
Prepared mustard
Vinegar
Salt and pepper
Sour cream

Use young dandelion leaves picked in the springtime when the flowers are still in bud; tear the leaves into small pieces. Using sharp scissors, cut some orange peel into the finest paper-thin strips possible. Boil the peel for 5 minutes in a saucepan with plenty of water to remove the bitterness; drain and chill. When cold, toss with the dandelion leaves. Mix all the seasonings to taste with the sour cream, pour over the dandelion leaves, mix and serve.

Egg Butterflies

2 hard-boiled eggs
4 large firm tomatoes
A little fresh mustard
A little watercress
Lettuce
Salad dressing (your choice)

Hard boil two eggs in a saucepan with plenty of water for 8–12 minutes. Drain, peel, cool, and cut into quarters. Wipe but do not skin the tomatoes. Place each one stem side down on individual salad plates; make a vertical cut down the center almost to the bottom, and a second vertical cut down each half almost to the bottom, making 4 wedges joined at the base. Spread them apart gently; place a slice of hard-boiled egg between each wedge, and garnish with a few mustard leaves and some watercress in the center. Serve on a bed of lettuce with the dressing on the side.

Stuffed Eggs

3 eggs
Mayonnaise
Pepper, salt, paprika
1 tomato
Lettuce and watercress

Hard boil the eggs in a saucepan with plenty of boiling water for 8–12 minutes. Turn them several times while they are cooking to keep the yolks in the center of the egg. Drain, peel and cut the eggs into halves lengthwise; carefully remove the yolks.

Mash and blend the yolks in a bowl with 2–3 heaping tablespoons of mayonnaise, or your favorite dressing, to make a smooth, creamy mixture. Season with pepper and salt and put in a pastry bag with a "rose" pattern tip. Place a small piece of tomato in the center of each egg half; then squeeze the yolk mixture through the rose tip of pastry bag to form a rose over the tomato. If you don't have a pastry bag, simply spoon a little of the yolk mixture into the center of the egg halves. Garnish with a little paprika and serve on a bed of lettuce or watercress.

Deviled Egg Salad

6 large eggs
2 tablespoons butter
2 tablespoons cream or mayonnaise
1 teaspoon French mustard
Dash of Worcestershire sauce
Salt and pepper
Parsley, capers or stuffed olives as garnish
Watercress or endive

Boil the eggs for 10 minutes in a saucepan with plenty of water; drain, peel, and cut into lengthwise halves; remove the yolks. Cream the butter in a bowl until it is very soft; then blend in the egg yolks, mayonnaise, mustard, and Worcestershire sauce; salt and pepper to taste. Beat until it is as smooth as icing. Put the yolk mixture into a pastry bag with a rose tip, and squeeze to make large rosettes on top of the egg white halves. Garnish with parsley, capers, or sliced stuffed olives. Put a heap of watercress or endive in the center of a round plate and surround with the filled eggs. Add a little red pepper or tomato slices as garnish to create a more colorful dish.

Egg and Cucumber Salad with Sour Cream

Whites of 3 hard-boiled eggs
3 tablespoons green onions
1 cucumber
Watercress or lettuce
1 cup sour cream
¾ teaspoon prepared mustard
½ teaspoon honey
4 teaspoons lemon juice
Salt and pepper
2 tablespoons olive oil
Garnish with mashed yolks of the
  hard-boiled eggs

Hard boil 3 eggs for 10 minutes in a saucepan with plenty of boiling water. Drain, peel, and remove the egg yolks. Finely chop the egg whites with the green onions; slice the cucumber, and mix together with the salad greens, using as much watercress or torn lettuce as you like. Cover and chill until needed. Blend the sour cream, mustard, honey, lemon juice, salt and pepper together in the blender, then slowly add the olive oil with the blender on a low speed. Put the dressing in a chilled bowl, sprinkle with crumbled egg yolks on top, and serve on the side with the salad.

Egg and Olive Salad

2 hard-boiled eggs
2 tablespoons ripe olives, chopped
2 tablespoons green pepper, diced
1 tablespoon chives, finely chopped
1 head of lettuce, shredded
½ cup salad oil
2 tablespoons white wine vinegar or
    lemon juice
3 teaspoons honey
1 teaspoon salt
½ teaspoon pepper
1 teaspoon paprika
1 teaspoon dry mustard
Garlic to taste, finely minced

Hard boil 2 eggs in a saucepan with plenty of boiling water for 10 minutes; drain, peel, and cool. Finely chop the eggs, olives, green pepper, and chives and toss together in a salad bowl with shredded lettuce. Blend the oil, lemon juice or vinegar, honey, salt, pepper, paprika, mustard, and garlic; shake well. Pour over the salad, toss again, and serve without delay.

Egg, Pear, and Raisin Salad

1 large (16-ounce) can of pears
2 tablespoons white wine vinegar
1 clove of garlic
2 iceberg lettuces with firm hearts
2 stalks of celery, finely chopped
½ cup walnuts, chopped
¾ cup raisins
2 hard-boiled eggs
4 tablespoons salad oil
1 teaspoon honey
1 level teaspoon salt
Dash of pepper

Drain and discard the pear syrup; place the pears into a bowl, pour the vinegar on top, and leave to soak while the rest of the salad is made. Rub the inside of a wooden salad bowl with a cut clove of garlic. Wash and shred the lettuce into the bowl, add the celery, walnuts, raisins, and sliced eggs, and toss well. Lift the pears carefully out of the vinegar and place on top of the salad. Blend together in a jar or the blender: the vinegar used to soak the pears, oil, honey, salt and pepper. Pour over the salad just before serving. Serves 9 to 10 people.

Endive Crown Salad

1 large cucumber, grated and drained
3 tablespoons mild onion, minced
4 tablespoons parsley, minced
1¼ cup (9 ounces) cream cheese
½ teaspoon salt
1 cup mayonnaise
½ teaspoon agar-agar powder or
    1 stick agar-agar
3 tablespoons cold water
Lettuce or endive
2 hard-boiled egg yolks, mashed
Radish as garnish

Peel and grate the cucumber; press through a sieve to drain off the excess liquid. Mince the onion and parsley, then mix together in a bowl with the cucumber, cream cheese, salt, and mayonnaise. Soften the agar-agar in 3 tablespoons of cold water; then dissolve it in the top of a double boiler over hot water. Cool to lukewarm, and blend well with the first mixture. Put into a deep springform pan with whole sprays of endive of an even height with perfect leaves placed around the sides of the pan to form a crown; chill until firm. Remove from the pan and serve on a bed of lettuce or endive. Sprinkle mashed, hard boiled egg yolk over top and garnish with radish roses.

Golden Glow Salad

1 packet lemon Jell-o
1 cup boiling water
1 cup canned pineapple juice
Pinch of salt
2 teaspoons lemon juice
1 medium (12-ounce) can crushed pineapple
1 medium carrot, grated
¾ cup nuts, chopped
Salad greens

Dissolve the Jell-o in a bowl with 1 cup of boiling water, add the pineapple juice and salt, and stir well. Add the lemon juice, stir once, and let it stand. When it becomes syrupy and begins to set, stir in the crushed pineapple, grated carrot, and nuts. Pour into a mold and chill in the refrigerator until quite firm. Serve on a bed of salad greens. Serves eight.

Molded Grape Salad

1 pound grapes
4 tablespoons French dressing
3 ounce packet of lemon Jell-o
2 cups hot water
5 tablespoons orange juice
3 tablespoons lemon juice
1 teaspoon onion juice
Good pinch of salt
6 tablespoons cream cheese (3 ounces)
Large lettuce leaves

Wash and cut the grapes into halves; remove the seeds. Set aside 24 of the grape halves. Marinate the remaining grapes in a bowl with the French dressing for ½ hour. Drain and keep the grapes and dressing separately. Dissolve the Jell-o in a bowl with 2 cups of hot water; stir in the lemon, orange, and onion juices; season with salt. Chill in the refrigerator until it begins to set. Then remove from the refrigerator and stir in the marinated grapes. Pour into a large 4-cup mold or divide into 6 individual molds (custard cups are ideal); chill until set.

Mash the cream cheese in a bowl until soft, then roll into 6 balls. Slightly flatten each cream cheese ball and place on top of the mold, and surround with a ring of grape halves, using the grapes you set aside. Serve on a bed of lettuce with mayonnaise on the side. Serves six.

Golden Salad

Lettuce
1 pound Jerusalem artichokes
3 hard-boiled eggs, separated
Pinch of parsley, finely chopped
Pinch of green onions or chives, finely chopped
1 teaspoon French mustard
1 tablespoon white wine vinegar
2 tablespoons olive oil
Salt and pepper

Wash and peel the Jerusalem artichokes; cook until tender over high heat in a saucepan with plenty of boiling, salted water. Add 3 eggs to the cooking artichokes and boil for 7–10 minutes until hard-boiled. Drain and refrigerate until cold. Peel and separate the egg whites from the egg yolks. Thinly slice the cold artichokes and arrange on a bed of lettuce leaves with the chopped egg whites, parsley, and chives. Sprinkle with a little vinegar to keep the artichokes white. Mash the egg yolks in a bowl and slowly stir in the mustard, vinegar, and oil; season to taste, stir until well-blended, and pour over the vegetables. Serve four.

Grape and Pear Salad

8 pear halves
Grape leaves
¾ cup (6 ounces) cream cheese
4 tablespoons cream
2 pounds seedless grapes
French dressing

Peel and cut into halves 4 fresh pears, or drain a can of pear halves. Place cut side down on a bed of grape leaves on individual salad plates. Blend the cream and cream cheese together in a bowl; spread generously over the sides and tops of the pears. Wash and cut the grapes into halves and place them close together, cut side down, on the covered pears, so that they resemble a bunch of grapes. If possible, put a piece of stem in the end of the pear. Serves eight.

Grapefruit and Lettuce Cup Salad

1 grapefruit
2 teaspoons honey
1 teaspoon French dressing
6 whole walnut halves
Lettuce

Use a sharp knife or scissors to cut the peel of the grapefruit into a "zigzag" cut around the middle. Be careful not to pierce the grapefruit "meat". Loosen the cut edges with the fingers; very gently and carefully, pull off half the skin, thus leaving the whole fruit in half the skin. Remove the fruit in one piece from the other half; gently pull the segments apart, peel off the skin, and remove the seeds. Replace the fruit into the cups made from the grapefruit skin and sprinkle with honey. Chill well. Sprinkle with dressing, garnish with walnuts, and serve on a bed of lettuce. Serves one.

Green Pepper Ring Salad

2 large green peppers, de-seeded and cut
* into rings*
2 medium onions, cut into rings
Endive and crisp romaine lettuce
½ cup French dressing

Arrange alternate rings of green pepper and onion on a bed of endive and shredded lettuce on 6 individual salad plates. Sprinkle with French dressing and serve.

Green Pea Salad

1½ cups (1½ pounds unshelled) green peas,
  cooked
3 hard-boiled eggs, sliced or chopped
3–4 stalks celery, diced
Lettuce
½ cup mayonnaise
1 cup peanuts, chopped
3 tomatoes, skinned and sliced

Shell the peas and cook for 10 minutes in a saucepan over high heat with 3 cups of boiling, salted water. If you do not have any hard-boiled eggs on hand, add 3 eggs to the boiling peas and cook for 10 minutes until hard-boiled. Drain and cool. Peel and chop the eggs in a bowl, add the cold peas and diced celery. Cover and chill. Spoon the pea mixture onto 6 individual salad plates, lined with lettuce leaves. Drop a spoonful of mayonnaise on top of each plate, and garnish with sliced tomatoes and peanuts.

Italian Salad

1 medium potato
2 small young turnips
2 medium carrots
¼ pound green beans
½ pound green peas
Mayonnaise
1 small tomato
6 olives, pitted and chopped
12 capers
2 tablespoons parsley, finely chopped
Garnish of hard-boiled eggs, sliced

Dice the potato, turnips, and carrots; chop the green beans into 1-inch lengths, and shell the peas. Cook together in a saucepan with plenty of boiling, salted water for 20 minutes, or until tender. If you do not have any hard-boiled eggs on hand, add 2 eggs to the boiling vegetables, and cook for 10 minutes until hard-boiled; lift out and chill. Drain the vegetables and chill together in a salad bowl. When chilled, blend with the mayonnaise, tomato, olives, capers, and parsley. Serve garnished with slices of hard-boiled eggs. In Italy, they would add anchovies, but the salad tastes fine without them.

Leek, Tomato, and Apple Salad

1 small leek (white part only)
1 small cooking apple
1 small yellow tomato
1 teaspoon lemon juice
½ teaspoon honey
1 tablespoon mayonnaise

Wash the leek well and cut into thin, crosswise slices. Skin, core, and dice the apple into small pieces. Peel and dice the tomato. Mix the vegetables and fruit together in a serving bowl; sprinkle with lemon juice, honey, and mayonnaise. Stir gently until well-blended and serve. Serves one.

Mushroom Salad

2 medium potatoes
⅓ pound raw button mushrooms
Watercress
4 stalks celery, diced
4 hard-boiled eggs, sliced
Mayonnaise

Cook the potatoes in a saucepan with plenty of boiling water for 20–30 minutes, until tender. Drain and chill; when cold, cut into slices. If you do not have any hard-boiled eggs on hand, add 4 eggs to the boiling potatoes and cook for 10 minutes until hard-boiled; lift out and chill. Set aside two of the eggs. Wash the mushrooms and cut into bite-size pieces if they are large; otherwise, use whole. Mix the mushrooms, watercress and diced celery together in a bowl, add the sliced eggs and potatoes last so that they do not crumble. Gently stir in enough mayonnaise to wet the mixture. Garnish with the slices of hard-boiled eggs, and serve.

Macaroni Cheese Salad

1½ cups uncooked macaroni
1 cut clove of garlic
1 medium (12-ounce) can of olives,
  pitted and chopped
3 stalks celery, diced
½ large green pepper, diced
6 tomatoes, cut in wedges
½ cup cheddar cheese, diced
French dressing

Cook the macaroni in a saucepan with boiling, salted water until just tender (15–20 minutes). Rub the inside of a wooden salad bowl with the cut garlic. Drain the macaroni, and mix with the next 5 ingredients in the salad bowl; coat with French dressing and stir until it glistens. Cover and chill for at least 1 hour. Serve on or with lettuce or other salad greens. Serves six to eight.

Mushroom and Olive Salad

½ teaspoon salt
2 teaspoons water
1 clove of garlic, minced
6 tablespoons salad oil
2 tablespoons vinegar
2 teaspoons lemon juice
1 teaspoon honey
½ teaspoon dry mustard
½ teaspoon rosemary
½ teaspoon Worcestershire sauce
1 small (4-ounce) can tiny button mushrooms,
   or ¼ pound fresh mushrooms

1 head of lettuce, torn into pieces
2–3 stalks celery, diced
4 green onions, chopped
1 heaping tablespoon parsley, minced
6 tablespoons stuffed olives, sliced

Dissolve the salt in a bowl with 2 teaspoons of water, add the garlic, and leave to stand for at least ½ hour; stir occasionally. Blend together in a blender the oil, vinegar, lemon juice, honey, mustard, rosemary, and Worcestershire sauce. Strain the garlic out of the water and blend the water with the dressing. Place the mushrooms in a bowl and pour the blended mixture over the top; then leave to stand for 20 minutes for the flavors to blend.

Toss the lettuce, celery, green onions, parsley, and olives together in a salad bowl; add the mushroom-dressing mixture and mix lightly. Serves 6.

Olive and Beet Mold

6 ounces lemon Jell-o
1 cup hot water
1 large (17-ounce) can beets, grated
12 stuffed olives, chopped
4 tablespoons gherkin pickles, chopped
2 teaspoons garlic powder
2 teaspoons onion salt
Lettuce
French dressing

Stir the Jell-o in a bowl with 1 cup of hot water, and when dissolved, add 1 cup of cold water. Drain the beets, adding the beet liquid to the Jell-o mix; chill the Jell-o until it begins to set. If the canned beets are whole, grate them. Remove the Jell-o from the refrigerator and blend in the olives, pickles, and beets; season with garlic and onion salt. Pour into a well-rinsed 6-inch square pan, or into rinsed individual molds (custard cups) and chill in the refrigerator until set. Serve on a dish lined with lettuce. Top with French dressing. Serves eight to ten.

Orange and Onion Salad

1 large orange
1 grapefruit
French dressing
"Glace" cherries
1 mild onion, cut into paper-thin rings
Watercress

Cut the orange and grapefruit into crosswise slices; then remove the peel and pits with kitchen scissors. (This is much easier than trying to cut neat slices when the skin has been removed.) Arrange on a chilled serving dish, sprinkle with French dressing; place a cherry in the center of each slice and garnish with the onion rings and watercress.

Oratava Salad

3 hard-boiled eggs
1½ cups cheddar cheese, grated
2 apples
Lemon juice
2 firm, ripe tomatoes
4 ripe bananas
Mayonnaise

Hard-boil 3 eggs in a saucepan with plenty of boiling water for 10 minutes, drain and chill. When chilled, peel and slice the eggs. Finely grate the cheese. Peel, core, and cut the apples into slices; place on a salad dish and sprinkle with a little lemon juice. Peel and slice the tomatoes. Cover the apple slices with slices of banana, and place alternate slices of tomato and egg around the edges of the dish. Pile the cheese in a mound in the middle of the dish and serve with mayonnaise.

Oriental Salad

½ cup salad oil
3 tablespoons tarragon or apple cider vinegar
3 tablespoons tomato ketchup
2 tablespoons honey
1 tablespoon lemon juice
¼ teaspoon salt and pepper
½ teaspoon paprika
¼ teaspoon garlic salt
½ pound (½ bunch) fresh young
    spinach leaves
6-ounce can bamboo shoots
6-ounce can water chestnuts
Fresh bean sprouts
1 hard-boiled egg
Sesame seeds

Blend by hand or in a blender: the oil, vinegar, ketchup, honey, lemon juice, salt, pepper, paprika, and garlic salt. Chill. Wash the spinach well, using first a warm rinse, then a cold rinse; towel dry. Tear into small pieces and place in a salad bowl. Thinly slice the water chestnuts and bamboo shoots and place in alternating layers with the bean sprouts on top of the bed of spinach. Pour the dressing over the salad and sprinkle with mashed egg and sesame seeds. Serves six.

Pears with Filbert and Cheese Balls

¾ cup minced filberts
1 cup (8 ounces) cream cheese
2 tablespoons maraschino cherry juice
Pinch of salt
8 fresh pears or
    2 large (17-ounce) cans of pear halves
Lemon juice if using fresh pears
1 romaine or red leaf lettuce

Bake the minced filberts in a shallow baking pan for 10–15 minutes at 300°F until lightly browned. Blend the cream cheese and cherry juice in a bowl, season with salt, and roll into balls the size of small marbles. Roll the balls in the toasted nuts. Arrange the pear halves on a large round dish with lettuce leaves. If fresh pears are used, dip them in lemon juice or they will turn brown. Place some of the cheese-nut balls in the cavities of the pears and use the rest as garnish around the pears. Serve with or without French dressing. Serves eight.

Pear Salad with Ginger Cheese

6 pear halves, canned or fresh
Lemon juice if using fresh pears
6 tablespoons (3 ounces) cream cheese
2 tablespoons cream
3 tablespoons crystallized or
  candied ginger, chopped
Watercress or endive

Drain and chill the pear halves. If using fresh pears, peel and core them first; then dip in lemon juice to keep them from turning brown. Blend the cream cheese with the cream in a bowl and add the finely chopped ginger. Arrange the pear halves, cut side up, on a serving plate lined with watercress or endive. Serve with a heaping spoonful of the ginger-cream cheese mix in the cavity of each pear half. Serves six.

Potter's Salad

1 precooked pastry shell (page 44)
1 cup (¼ pound) cooked young carrots
2 pears
4 tablespoons (2 ounces) cream cheese
4 tomatoes
Dressing

If you do not have a precooked pastry shell, then first prepare one and chill. Boil the carrots in a saucepan with plenty of water for 20 minutes until tender. Drain, chill, and cut into slices. Peel, core and cut the pears into halves. Place them in the pastry shell, cut sides up, and fill the hollows with cream cheese. Skin and slice the tomatoes, and arrange the slices with the carrots in the spaces between the pears. Dot with dressing or mayonnaise and serve.

Potato Salad Roll

5 medium new potatoes
2–3 stalks celery, finely sliced
3 tablespoons sweet pickle, finely chopped
2 tablespoons parsley, minced
2 tablespoons pimiento, minced
4 hard boiled eggs, chopped
2 teaspoons onion, grated
Salt
Paprika
2 teaspoons lemon juice
Mayonnaise
Radish roses
Parsley for garnish

Boil the potatoes in a saucepan with plenty of water for 30–40 minutes, until tender. Drain, chill, and cut into 1-inch cubes. If you don't already have hard-boiled eggs on hand, add 4 eggs to the boiling potatoes for 15 minutes, remove, and chill. Mix the first six ingredients together in a bowl and season with onion, salt, paprika, and lemon juice. Add enough mayonnaise to bind the salad together, and place the mixture on a piece of aluminum foil. Shape into a roll 8 x 4 x 2½-inches and roll up in the foil. Refrigerate for 24 hours. Discard the foil wrapping and serve garnished with radish roses, or, put stiff mayonnaise on top as an icing and garnish with parsley. Cut in slices to serve. Serves eight.

Sliced Potato Salad

6 medium potatoes
2 green onions, minced
3 tablespoons mayonnaise
Lettuce
Parsley, finely chopped
Mustard and Watercress

Boil the potatoes in a saucepan with plenty of water for 30–40 minutes, until tender. Drain, chill, and cut into slices. Blend the minced onions with the mayonnaise, and gently mix with the sliced potatoes. Pile on a serving dish lined with lettuce, sprinkle generously with parsley, and garnish with mustard and watercress.

Sour Cream and Potato Salad

4 medium potatoes
1 small cucumber, diced
2 teaspoons mild onion, minced
½ teaspoon celery seed
1½ teaspoons Sea salt

3 hard boiled eggs

1 cup sour cream
¼ cup vinegar
1 teaspoon prepared mustard
4 tablespoons salad dressing or mayonnaise
Lettuce or other salad greens
Grated cheese (your choice)

Boil the potatoes in a saucepan with plenty of water for 30–40 minutes, until tender. Drain, chill, and dice. If you don't already have boiled eggs on hand, add three eggs to the boiling potatoes, cook 15 minutes, remove, and chill. Gently toss first five ingredients together in a bowl. Separate the egg yolks from the whites, dice the whites, and add to the first ingredients. Mash the egg yolks in a separate bowl, and blend in the sour cream, mustard, vinegar, and mayonnaise. Add the dressing to the potato mixture and stir gently. Leave to stand in a cold place for 15 minutes to allow the flavors to blend. Serve on a bed of lettuce or other greens, sprinkled with grated cheese.

Rice and Green Pea Salad

1 level teaspoon turmeric
2 cups vegetable stock (page 11)
1 cup uncooked brown rice, short or long grain
2½ cups (2½ pounds unhulled) peas
4 green onions, minced
4 tablespoons olive oil
Garnish of chopped chives or parsley

Mix the turmeric with the stock in a large saucepan and bring to a boil over heat; add the rice, cover, and cook at the lowest possible heat for 45 minutes, then remove the lid and cook until the excess liquid has evaporated. (Be careful to not let it burn!) Pour the rice into a large bowl and leave to cool. Boil the peas in ½ cup water in a covered saucepan for 15 minutes, until just tender. Drain and chill. Mix together all the ingredients, except the garnish, in a bowl and coat with the oil. Garnish with chives or parsley on top, cover, refrigerate for 15 minutes, and serve. No more dressing is needed. Serves eight.

Rosy Salad

½ cup lemon juice
4 cloves
1½ tablespoons honey
½ teaspoon salt
5–6 small beets
6 hard boiled eggs

Mix the lemon juice, cloves, honey, and salt in a saucepan. Peel and slice the beets into the saucepan and mix well. Cook over very low heat for 10 minutes, then let cool. In a separate saucepan, boil 6 eggs in plenty of water for 15 minutes, drain, chill, and slice. Pile the beets on a serving dish lined with lettuce. Garnish with the sliced eggs, cover and chill to serve very cold.

Russian Salad

2 potatoes
⅓ cup (⅓ pound unhulled) green peas
3 carrots, thinly sliced
¾ cup (¼ pound) green string beans, diced
Salt and pepper
1 teaspoon lemon juice
2–3 tablespoons mayonnaise

Boil the potatoes in a saucepan with plenty of water for 30–40 minutes, until tender. Drain, chill, and dice. Simmer the hulled peas in ½ cup water in a saucepan over medium heat for 15 minutes, until just tender. Drain and cool. If the carrots and beans are very young they may be used raw; otherwise boil them in a saucepan with plenty of water for 15 minutes, until just tender. Mix all the ingredients together in a bowl, season to taste, sprinkle with lemon juice, and bind with mayonnaise. Serves two.

Salade de Panais

4 young parsnips
¼ pound (¼ cup) green peas
4–5 stalks celery hearts, sliced
Mayonnaise
Lettuce

Peel and cook the parsnips with the peas over medium heat in a saucepan with 1 cup of water for 15–20 minutes, until just tender. Drain and chill. Cut the parsnips crosswise into ½-inch thick slices, and cut out the cores if they are at all hard. Toss all the ingredients together in a bowl, moisten with mayonnaise, and serve on a generous bed of crisp lettuce.

Spanish Salad

3 hard boiled eggs
1 large garlic clove, peeled
3 slices French bread, toasted
1 romaine lettuce
3 tablespoons ripe olives, minced
French dressing

Boil 3 eggs for 15 minutes in a pan with plenty of water; drain and chill. Rub the cut garlic on the toasted bread slices, and cut the toast into small cubes. Peel and finely chop the

hard-boiled eggs. Wash and towel dry the lettuce, tear into bite-size pieces, and place in a salad bowl. Add the egg, toast, and olives; sprinkle with the dressing and toss gently.

Spinach Salad with Nut Dressing

¾ cup nuts (pine, cashew or walnut)
3 tablespoons olive oil
3 tablespoons tarragon vinegar
¼ teaspoon grated lemon rind
¼ teaspoon salt
Dash of nutmeg
1–2 bunches young spinach leaves

Mix the nuts, olive oil, vinegar, lemon rind, salt, and nutmeg together in a salad bowl. Wash the spinach leaves twice using first a warm rinse, then a cold rinse. Towel dry and tear into bite-size pieces. Add to the nut dressing and toss. Serves six.

Tomato and Avocado Salad

4 tomatoes
4 tablespoons olive or salad oil
4 tablespoons lemon juice
2 large avocados
¼ teaspoon salt
1 clove garlic, cut in half
1 head of lettuce
6 stalks of chicory (optional)
1 head of endive (optional)
Dressing

Peel and cut the tomatoes into eighths. Place in a small bowl with two tablespoons each of the oil and the lemon juice over the top, cover, and chill. Cut the avocados into halves lengthwise, remove the pits and peel. Cut into crescent-shaped slices, place in a bowl, and sprinkle with the rest of the oil, lemon juice, and salt. Rub a wooden salad bowl with the cut garlic and shred the salad greens into the bowl. Add the tomatoes and avocado and mix carefully. Sprinkle dressing over the top. Serves six to eight.

Jellied Tomatoes

1 tablespoon green peas
1 tablespoon carrot
1 tablespoon chicory
½ teaspoon agar-agar powder or
   1 stick agar-agar
1 cup vegetable stock or water (page 11)
3 large tomatoes
1 large, crisp head of lettuce
1 tablespoon parsley or chervil, chopped

Cook a handful of peas, chicory, and 1 carrot in a saucepan with 1 cup of water over medium heat for 15–20 minutes until just tender. Drain and chill; dice the carrot and chicory. Dissolve the agar-agar in the stock. Cut the tomatoes in half crosswise, scoop out the pulp and seeds; mash the pulp, add to the stock and agar-agar, and refrigerate. Chill the tomato halves. When the jelly is almost set, add the peas, diced carrots, and chicory; then chill again until firm. Spoon the jelly into the tomato halves, piling it up as high as possible. Serve each tomato on individual serving plates on a bed of lettuce leaves, garnished with parsley or chervil. Serve very cold. Serves six.

Stuffed Tomato Salad

½ cup uncooked rice
5 large tomatoes
1 onion, grated
Some stuffed olives
Salad dressing
Salt and pepper
5 mushrooms
Butter, seasoned with garlic
Lettuce
Watercress

Precook the rice in a covered saucepan with 1 cup of boiling water over low heat for 30–40 minutes until tender. Chill. Cut the tops off the tomatoes and scoop out the pulp. Chop the pulp and mix it with the grated onion and a few chopped olives in a bowl; add the chilled rice and bind with salad dressing; season to taste. Fill the tomato halves with this mixture. Lightly sauté the whole mushrooms in a frying pan with butter seasoned with garlic. Place the tomatoes in a ring on a dish lined with lettuce leaves, and arrange the mushrooms in between the tomatoes, caps up. Garnish the tomatoes with some sliced olives and watercress.

Tomato Rose Salad

8 firm, medium tomatoes
1½ cups (12 ounces) cream cheese
Milk
2 hard boiled egg yolks
Lettuce leaf cups
French dressing
Watercress

Peel and chill the tomatoes. Soften the cream cheese in a bowl with enough milk to make a creamy but firm consistency (you do not want this to be "runny"). Press a small teaspoon filled level with the cream cheese and milk mixture against the side of the tomato then draw it down with a curving motion to make a petal shape. If the mixture is too soft the petals will not stay in place. It is a good idea to try this out on a potato or some other round object until you can make the petals with ease. Cover each tomato with petals. Sprinkle the center of each "rose" tomato with mashed egg yolk. Put each "rose" on a lettuce leaf formed into a cup shape and garnish with a few watercress leaves. Serve with French dressing. Do not be discouraged if you do not make a perfect rose the first time. Practice makes perfect! Serves eight.

Tropical Salad

1 medium cabbage
1¼ cups flaked coconut
1 cup (½ pint) sour cream
2 tablespoons vinegar or lemon juice
½ teaspoon salt
3 teaspoons honey
Toasted coconut
Paprika

Finely shred the cabbage and mix with the flaked coconut in a salad bowl. Blend the sour cream, vinegar, salt, and honey in a blender; pour over the cabbage mixture and toss well. Spread a thin layer of coconut on a cookie sheet and bake in a preheated oven at 350°F for 3–4 minutes. Watch carefully as it burns easily. Sprinkle toasted coconut and paprika over the salad and serve.

Valentine Salad

1 teaspoon agar-agar powder or
  1 stick agar-agar
½ cup cold water
1 large (17-ounce) can Italian tomatoes
2 teaspoons onion, minced
½ teaspoon celery seed
6 tablespoons cream cheese
1 teaspoon lemon juice
Endive
French dressing

Soften the agar-agar in ½ cup cold water. Dice the tomatoes and heat together with the onion, celery seed, and cream cheese in a saucepan over medium heat for 15 minutes. Strain the softened agar-agar into the hot mixture, add the lemon juice, and set aside to cool. Pour into five heart-shaped molds and chill until firm. If you do not have heart-shaped molds, then pour the jelly into a shallow pan, and when set, cut the heart-shapes with a biscuit cutter. Toss the endive with a little dressing and arrange it on six salad plates; place a jellied tomato heart on each one and serve. Serves six.

Vegetable Mayonnaise Salad

2 beets
½ cup (½ pound unhulled) green peas
4 potatoes
2 carrots
1 hard boiled egg
¼ medium cauliflower
4 gherkin pickles
1 small (8¾-ounce) can beans your choice,
   drained
Salad dressing or mayonnaise
Lettuce
Watercress
Celery, sliced and curled

Boil the beets in a saucepan with 2 cups of water for 20 minutes until just tender. Drain, chill, and slice. Hull and cook the peas in a separate saucepan with ½ cup of water over medium heat for 20 minutes until just tender. Drain and chill. Boil the potatoes and carrots together in a saucepan with plenty of water for 30–40 minutes until tender. Drain and chill. Boil an egg with the potatoes for 15 minutes, lift out and chill. Steam the cauliflower in a covered saucepan with a steam rack and ½ cup of water for 15 minutes until just tender, but still crisp. Drain and divide into florets. Dice the potatoes and carrots, chop the gherkins and egg, and mix them all together with the peas and beans in a bowl; bind with mayonnaise. Line a salad bowl with lettuce leaves, pile the vegetables in, and garnish with watercress. Arrange the slices of beets and celery curls as garnish around the edge of the salad.

Walnut and Cabbage Salad

1 small cabbage
1 avocado, diced
1 carrot, grated
1¼ cups walnuts, chopped
4 green onions, diced
Garlic salt

½ cup mayonnaise
½ tablespoon prepared mustard
Juice of 1 lemon
A little grated lemon rind

Finely shred the cabbage and mix with the next five ingredients in a bowl. Blend the mayonnaise, mustard, and lemon juice together in a blender, or by hand, and toss with the salad. Serve in a bowl with the grated lemon rind on top. Serves six.

Yogurt and Cucumber Salad

1 large cucumber
1 cup yogurt
4 teaspoons mint, freshly chopped
Salt to taste

Peel and thinly slice the cucumber with a potato peeler. Blend the yogurt, mint, and salt in a bowl. (Add a touch of garlic, if you like.) Add the cucumber slices and chill for at least 1 hour before serving. Serves four to five.

Zucchini Salad

3 small zucchini
4 tablespoons olive oil
2 cloves of garlic, crushed
Mixed salad greens
Garnish of minced green onions
4 tablespoons Parmesan cheese
French dressing

Wipe the zucchini, slice crosswise into 1-inch pieces, and discard the end pieces. Steam in a covered saucepan with a steam rack over boiling water for 2 minutes, drain and place the pieces on a plate. Be careful not to let them overlap or they will become limp. Leave to cool, then refrigerate for 15 minutes. Fifteen minutes before serving, mix the oil and garlic, and pour over the zucchini to marinate for a few minutes. Mix carefully in a salad bowl with the chosen salad greens, adding French dressing if desired. Garnish with minced green onions and Parmesan cheese.

Chapter Five—Salad Dressings

Chapter Five—Salad Dressings

Basic Salad Dressing #1

2 teaspoons arrowroot or cornstarch
1 teaspoon salt
1 teaspoon pepper
1 teaspoon dry mustard
½ cup water
1 tablespoon margarine, melted
1 teaspoon honey
1 raw egg yolk
Vinegar to taste

Mix the arrowroot, salt, pepper, and dry mustard in a saucepan; blend with ½ cup of water, and cook and stir over medium high heat until the mixture boils. Remove from the heat, add the margarine, honey, and raw egg yolk, and whisk well. Add the vinegar by drops, to taste, stirring until well-blended.

Basic Salad Dressing #2

1 cup white sauce (page 121)
1 tablespoon vinegar
1 teaspoon salt
1 teaspoon pepper
1 teaspoon dry mustard
1 teaspoon honey

Beat the vinegar into the white sauce in a bowl. Mix together the salt, pepper, and mustard; add, with the honey, to the sauce. Beat vigorously. Taste and adjust the vinegar to taste.

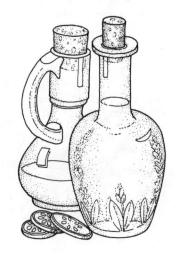

Variations of the Basic Salad Dressing

Chili Salad Dressing

Chili sauce
Vinegar
Worcestershire sauce
Garlic
Chives

To 1 cup of salad dressing add: 1 cup chili sauce, 2 tablespoons vinegar, 3 tablespoons Worcestershire sauce, and a heaping teaspoon of chopped garlic or chives.

Chutney Salad Dressing

To 1 cup of salad dressing add 1 tablespoon of chutney and mix well.

Red Salad Dressing

Tinge the dressing #1 or #2 with tomato ketchup!

Watercress Salad Dressing

¼ pound watercress
1 clove of garlic, mashed
2 teaspoons lemon juice
Salt

Blend all the above ingredients in an electric blender with 1 cup of basic salad dressing. Blend until the watercress is finely minced.

Boiled Salad Dressing

1 teaspoon whole wheat flour
1 teaspoon dry mustard
Salt and pepper
1 whole egg, beaten
Dash of honey
2 tablespoons salad oil
2 cups boiling water
Vinegar

Mix the flour, mustard, salt and pepper in the top of a double boiler over boiling water. Add the beaten egg and honey and, when well-blended, add the salad oil. Now add the boiling water very slowly, stirring all the time. Then add a little vinegar, a few drops at a time, to taste. Cook and stir in the top of the double boiler until the mixture thickens.

Salad Dressing Without Oil or Egg #1

1 level teaspoon salt
2 teaspoons prepared mustard
1 small (8¾-ounce) can evaporated milk
1 tablespoon honey
3 tablespoons vinegar

Mix the salt and mustard in a bowl, then slowly stir in the undiluted canned milk and honey. Mix well and add the vinegar drop by drop. When well-blended pour into clean, dry bottles with screw tops or corks. Will keep for several weeks. If it tastes too strong, add water.

Salad Dressing Without Oil or Egg #2

7 teaspoons margarine, melted
2 tablespoons whole wheat flour
Salt and pepper
1 cup milk
Vinegar

Put 4 teaspoons of the margarine into the top of a double boiler over boiling water; stir in the flour, and season with salt and pepper. Stir in the milk slowly and cook for a few minutes, stirring all the time, until the mixture thickens and the "raw" taste is gone. Remove from the heat, leave to cool, and stir in the remaining 3 teaspoons of melted margarine; then add, drop by drop, vinegar to taste.

Cooked Salad Dressing (For Storing)

4 tablespoons margarine, melted
5 tablespoons whole wheat flour
1 tablespoon arrowroot or cornstarch
1 teaspoon dry mustard
3 cups milk, heated
2 teaspoons honey
1 level teaspoon salt
1 raw egg, well-beaten
Vinegar to taste

Mix the margarine, flour, arrowroot, and mustard together in a saucepan; then stir in the milk. Stir until well-mixed; then add the honey and salt. Boil gently over medium-high heat, stirring constantly, until the mixture thickens and is quite smooth. Remove from the heat, let cool; then stir in the beaten egg and cook very gently over low heat, just to reheat; do not let it boil. Remove from the heat, cover, and let cool again; then add the vinegar, drop by drop, to taste.

American Salad Dressing

1 level teaspoon salt
1 level teaspoon dry mustard
2 tablespoons whole wheat flour
1 raw egg, beaten
2 teaspoons honey
2 tablespoons butter or margarine, melted
½ cup milk
¼ cup vinegar

Mix the salt, mustard, and flour in the top of a double boiler. Stir the beaten egg and honey into the flour mixture; then stir in the melted butter and milk, and cook over hot water until thickened, stirring all the time. Remove from the heat and drop in the vinegar very slowly; beat well. Strain and leave to cool. Bottle and cap tightly.

Cottage Cheese Salad Dressing

4 tablespoons cottage cheese
½ cup evaporated milk
½ cup lemon juice
2 teaspoons honey
¼ teaspoon salt
Dash of paprika
2 teaspoons chives, chopped

Beat all the ingredients together in a bowl until smooth. Bottle and cap tightly.

Three Cheeses Salad Dressing

1 cup (4 ounces) blue cheese
1 cup (8 ounces) cream cheese
3 tablespoons sharp cheese, grated
½ teaspoon fresh tarragon
½ teaspoon salt
Dash of pepper
½ clove of garlic, mashed or
    ½ teaspoon garlic powder
4 tablespoons milk

Blend the cheeses together in a small bowl using an electric mixer. Add the tarragon, salt, pepper, and garlic; mix again. Beat in the milk at slow speed until the mixture is smooth but not thin.

Citrus Dressing

4 tablespoons honey
4 tablespoons tarragon vinegar
4 tablespoons tomato ketchup
1 level teaspoon salt
1 small onion, grated
1 clove of garlic, minced
1 cup salad oil

Mix all the ingredients in a bottle with a lid, cover, and shake well. Chill before using.

Lemon or Lime French Dressing

½ cup salad or olive oil
½ cup lemon or lime juice
¼ teaspoon salt
Dash of pepper
4 teaspoons honey

Put all the ingredients into a jar with a lid and shake well.

Basic French Dressing

1 teaspoon pepper
3 tablespoons vinegar (wine vinegar if possible)
½ cup olive oil
1 teaspoon salad oil

Mix the pepper and vinegar together in a quart bottle with a lid, add both the oils, and shake well. Some people like to add a little honey and lemon juice instead of vinegar. Always shake well before using.

Variations of the Basic French Dressing

Caper French Dressing

Add 3 tablespoons of capers to the basic French dressing.

Chiffonade French Dressing

Add 2 teaspoons each of chopped cooked beets, chopped chives, and hard boiled eggs to the basic French dressing.

Tarragon French Dressing

Use tarragon vinegar instead of plain vinegar in the basic French dressing.

Fine Herbs French Dressing

Add 2 teaspoons each of minced parsley, watercress, chervil, and basil to the basic French dressing.

Vinaigrette

Add 1 tablespoon each of chopped chives and chopped sweet pickle to the basic French dressing.

Zippy French Dressing

½ teaspoon salt
Dash of pepper
¼ teaspoon dry mustard
1 teaspoon Worcestershire sauce
1 tablespoon onion, finely minced
1 clove of garlic or
  1 teaspoon garlic powder or granules
2 tablespoons wine vinegar
6 tablespoons olive or salad oil

Mix all the ingredients together in a bowl and beat with a whisk until blended. Store in a jar with a lid and shake well before using.

Jane's Sesame Seed Dressing

2 cloves of garlic
½ teaspoon salt
1 cup olive or salad oil
½ cup vinegar
½ cup cream
2 teaspoons sesame seeds
Pepper

Chop the garlic and mix with the salt; then mix all the ingredients together in a large jar and shake well. Leave overnight so that the flavors may blend. This is especially good with cabbage salad.

Cup French Dressing

1 cup salad or olive oil
¼ cup vinegar
½ teaspoon salt
Pepper
2 tablespoons parsley, chopped

Mix the ingredients together in a quart jar with a lid and shake well before using.

Low Calorie French Dressing

1 cup cider vinegar
1 tablespoon tomato ketchup
2 tablespoons honey
1 tablespoon chili sauce
4 tablespoons water
½ teaspoon garlic, minced
½ teaspoon dry mustard
¼ teaspoon paprika
¼ teaspoon black pepper
1 teaspoon salt

This dressing is appealing to weight-watchers, as there is no oil in the ingredients. Put all the ingredients into a jar and shake well. If it is too strong, add more water.

Mayonnaise

However good the ingredients of a salad may be, they can always be enhanced with a dressing to bind them, to blend the flavors into a harmonious whole.

Possibly the best known of all salad dressings is mayonnaise. Although experienced cooks sometimes flinch at making mayonnaise, it need not be terrifying. It does, however, need patience to make in the conventional way. An electric blender makes a perfect mayonnaise with ease.

Blender Mayonnaise

1 cup olive oil
1 level teaspoon French mustard
1 teaspoon salt
Dash of pepper
4 teaspoons white wine vinegar
2 raw egg yolks

Add all the ingredients one at a time into the blender in the order given. Chill.

Basic Mayonnaise

2 raw egg yolks
1 teaspoon salt
1 teaspoon black pepper freshly ground
1 cup olive oil
1 level teaspoon French mustard
2 teaspoons tarragon vinegar or
  2 teaspoons white wine vinegar
Juice of ½ small lemon, strained
½ cup cream

Chill the blender jar. Drop in the egg yolks, French mustard, salt and pepper; blend at medium slow speed until creamy and well-blended. Then, still blending, drip the oil in slowly until the mixture thickens. Now, but not before, add a few drops of the wine vinegar and the rest of the oil, blending at a slightly faster speed. Blend in the remaining vinegar, drop in the lemon juice, and lastly, add the cream. If the mayonnaise is too thick, drop in a little more vinegar.

If you do not have a blender, combine the above ingredients in the order given, using a chilled bowl and egg beater.

A lighter and more digestible mayonnaise may be made if the egg white is beaten stiffly and folded in just before the mayonnaise is to be used. If, in spite of all your care, the mayonnaise curdles you can "save" it by putting a few drops of very hot water in a bowl; add a few drops of the curdled mixture, and whisk; continue to add the faulty mayonnaise a little at a time and whisk until it is creamy again.

Variations of the Basic Mayonnaise Dressing

Appetizer Mayonnaise

1 cup chili sauce
1 teaspoon Worcestershire sauce
1 teaspoon prepared horseradish
2 minced pickles
1 stalk of celery, minced
2 teaspoons chives, minced
4 teaspoons parsley, minced

To 1 cup of the basic mayonnaise beat in the above ingredients in the order given.

Bar-Le-Duc Mayonnaise

To the basic mayonnaise add 3 tablespoons of red currant jelly and 2 teaspoons lemon juice.

Fluffy Horseradish Mayonnaise

6 tablespoons whipped cream
3 tablespoons prepared horseradish
4 drops Tabasco sauce

Add the above ingredients to the basic mayonnaise and blend well.

Cheese Mayonnaise

To the basic mayonnaise add 6 tablespoons (3 ounces) cream cheese and 2 tablespoons of Camembert cheese. Blend well. This is especially good with potato or egg salads.

Cream Cheese Mayonnaise

6 tablespoons (3 ounces) cream cheese
2 teaspoons lemon juice
2 tablespoons toasted almonds, chopped
6 tablespoons whipped cream

Add the above ingredients to the basic mayonnaise and blend well.

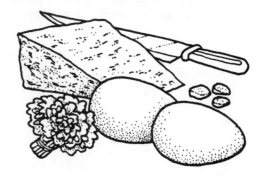

Mayonnaise Without Oil

2 tablespoons whole wheat flour
1½ teaspoons dry mustard
1 teaspoon salt
Dash of pepper
1 tablespoon margarine, melted
2 teaspoons honey
1 raw egg yolk, beaten
½ cup milk
2 tablespoons vinegar
1 egg white, stiffly beaten

In the top of a double boiler mix the flour, mustard, salt and pepper; add the melted margarine, honey, beaten egg yolk, milk, and vinegar. Whisk well. Cook over hot water and stir until the mixture thickens. Remove from the heat, cover, and leave to cool; then fold in the stiffly beaten egg white. Store in a covered jar in a cold place. This is a perfect dressing for those on restricted oil diets.

Mayonnaise Without Egg

1 small potato
1 level teaspoon prepared mustard
Salt
2 teaspoons vinegar
½ cup olive or salad oil

Steam the potato in its skin for 20 minutes in a saucepan with a steam rack. Drain, cool, peel, and mash in a bowl. Add the mustard, salt to taste, and very slowly beat in the vinegar; then beat in the oil a few drops at a time. Ideal for those who are allergic to eggs.

Tartar Sauce

4 hard boiled egg yolks
Pinch of salt
Few drops of vinegar
Juice of a finely grated onion
1½ cups olive oil
Chives

Boil 4 eggs in a saucepan with plenty of water for 15 minutes. Drain, chill, and separate the yolks from the whites. Mash the yolks, mix in a good pinch of salt and a few drops of vinegar, and blend to a smooth paste. Press out the juice of a finely grated onion into a bowl, using a garlic press; add the egg yolks and then the olive oil, drop by drop, stirring constantly. When well-blended add a little chopped chives. For a variation on this, add some sweet relish.

Thousand Island Mayonnaise

4 tablespoons chili sauce
4 teaspoons stuffed olives, chopped
1 teaspoon capers, chopped
1 teaspoon chives, chopped

Add the above ingredients to 1 cup of the basic mayonnaise and blend well.

Chapter Six—Desserts and Puddings

Chapter Six—Desserts and Puddings

Ambrosia

2 tablespoons butter
⅔ cup rolled oats
⅓ cup mixed nuts, chopped
2½ tablespoons honey
1 cup corn flakes
⅛ cup walnuts, chopped
⅓ cup raisins
1 cup Half and Half

Melt the butter in a thick frying pan over low heat, add the oats and the mixed nuts, and cook until lightly brown. Stir from time to time or they will burn. Add the honey and cook for 3–5 more minutes, stirring all the time. Transfer to a mixing bowl, add the corn flakes, walnuts, and raisins. Mix well and serve cold with Half and Half or cream.

Anne's Aniseed Cookies

8 tablespoons (1 cube) butter
⅓ cup honey
1 egg
⅔ cup self-rising flour
Pinch of salt
1 cup rolled oats
1½ cups desiccated coconut
2 teaspoons aniseed

Preheat oven to 350°F

Cream the butter and honey in a bowl, add the egg, and beat well. Sift the flour and salt into the creamed mixture and stir. Mix the oats, coconut, and aniseed together in a separate bowl, then add to the first mixture and stir well to a thick consistency. Roll into small balls, arrange on a greased cookie sheet, and bake at 350°F for 12–15 minutes. Cool on the cookie sheets and store.

Apple Tart

PASTRY:
1 cup whole wheat flour
6 tablespoons margarine or butter
1 egg
¼ cup honey
2 tablespoons milk

FILLING:
1 tablespoon bread crumbs
¾ pound (2 medium-sized) cooking apples
¼ cup raisins
⅓ cup honey
Cinnamon

Preheat oven to 400°F

Sift the flour into a bowl and finely cut in the butter using a pastry cutter. Beat the egg slightly, put a little aside for the top of the tart, and add the rest, with ¼ cup of honey, to the flour. Stir in enough milk to make a damp dough. Mix to a ball and leave to stand for 30 minutes. Cut the pastry ball in half, and roll out one half to form a pie crust. Place in a pie pan and bake for 15 minutes at 400°F.

Layer the bottom of the baked pastry shell with bread crumbs; then peel, core, and slice the apples into the baked pastry shell. Add the raisins and pour ⅓ cup of honey on top.

Roll out the other piece of pastry, dampen the edge of the lower pastry, and cover it with the top layer; press on the rim to seal, trim neatly, paint the top with the reserved egg, and sprinkle with a little cinnamon. Bake for 30–40 minutes at 400°F. This is tasty served either hot or cold.

Apple Pudding

FILLING:
1 pound (2–3 medium-sized) cooking apples
4 cloves
2 tablespoons seedless raisins
1 tablespoon lemon juice
1 tablespoon honey

BATTER:
2 cups whole wheat flour
Pinch of salt
⅓ cup honey
2 eggs
2 cups milk

Preheat oven to 350°F

Peel, core, and slice the apples into the bottom of a greased 8 x 8-inch baking dish. Add the cloves and raisins, sprinkle with lemon juice, and dab with honey. Mix the batter ingredients together in a bowl, and pour over the apples. Bake at 350°F for 1 hour.

Filled Apricots

2 fresh apricots
1 tablespoon whipped cream
1 heaping tablespoon grated nuts
⅔ teaspoon honey
A little grated chocolate (optional)

Cut the apricots in halves and remove the pits. Mix the other ingredients together and fill the hollows of the apricots. Chill and serve. Serves one.

Sweet Apricots

¼ pound dried apricots
2 cups milk
1 tablespoon honey
1 teaspoon lemon juice

Wash and cut the apricots into quarters. Warm the milk and honey together in a saucepan over low heat until the honey is dissolved, but do not boil. Pour over the apricots in a bowl and leave to cool. When cold, sprinkle with the lemon juice. Leave to stand for at least 12 hours.

Banana Bread

1⅔ cups self-rising flour
½ teaspoon baking soda
¼ teaspoon Sea salt
¼ teaspoon ground cardamom
¼ teaspoon ground mace
8 tablespoons (1 cube) margarine
⅓ cup honey
2 eggs
¼ teaspoon vanilla extract
3 ripe bananas, mashed
¾ cup walnuts, chopped

Preheat oven to 350°F

Sift together the flour, baking soda, salt, and spices several times. Cream the margarine and honey in a bowl, beat in the eggs and vanilla extract, then stir in the flour mix and mashed bananas alternately. Stir the nuts in last. Pour the mixture into a greased and floured bread pan, and bake at 350°F for 1 hour. Do not turn out of the pan until the banana bread is cold. Serve in slices, buttered.

Christmas Cake

1 cup glacé cherries
1 cup golden raisins (sultanas)
1 cup seedless raisins
1 cup crystallized pineapple
1 cup glacé figs
1 cup mixed peel
1 cup shelled almonds

1 cup whole wheat flour
2 tablespoons self-rising flour
1 teaspoon cinnamon
1 teaspoon ground cloves
1 teaspoon allspice
1 teaspoon nutmeg
1 level teaspoon salt

8 tablespoons (1 cube) margarine
¾ cup honey
5 eggs
Juice and grated rind of 1 lemon
½ cup rum or ½ cup orange juice

Preheat oven to 300°F

Cut the glacé cherries into halves, and chop the larger fruit into small pieces; mix together in a bowl with the mixed peel and almonds. Sift the flour, spices, and salt together in a bowl; then add a cupful of the fruit mix. In a separate large bowl, cream the margarine and honey; beat in the eggs, one at a time, then add the lemon juice and grated lemon rind. Fold in the flour, then the fruit mixture, and finally the rum or orange juice. Line an 8-inch cake pan with 2 layers of brown paper and 1 layer of greased wax paper. Pour the cake mixture into the pan, smooth the top, and bake at 300°F for 4 hours.

Coriander Apple Crumble

3–4 apples
1 tablespoon honey
1 teaspoon cinnamon
⅓ cup honey
10 tablespoons butter or margarine, softened
1 cup flour
1 teaspoon crushed coriander seeds

Preheat oven to 350°F

Peel, core, and slice the apples into the bottom of a greased 8 x 8-inch baking dish. Dab with honey and sprinkle with cinnamon. Blend ⅓ cup of honey with the margarine in a bowl, stir in the flour, and cover the top of the apples. Sprinkle with crushed coriander seeds and bake at 350°F for ½ hour.

Variation: For a yummy variation of this recipe, substitute oats for the flour and add a dash of lemon juice.

Christmas Pudding

1 stick agar-agar or
  ¾ teaspoon agar-agar powder
Warm water
10 ounces of mixed dried fruit
1 teaspoon mixed spice
¼ teaspoon ground ginger
¼ teaspoon grated nutmeg
1 tablespoon cocoa or unsweetened chocolate
  powder
2 tablespoons honey
1½ cups water
8 tablespoons strained orange juice
1 tablespoon sherry
3 ounces orange or lemon peel, chopped
Whipping cream

Soften the agar-agar in a few tablespoons of warm water in a bowl. Put the fruit, spices, chocolate powder, and honey into a saucepan; add 1½ cups of water and the orange juice, and boil over high heat for 5 minutes. Remove from the heat, add the softened agar-agar, sherry, and lemon peel; mix well. Rinse a 7½-inch ring mold with cold water, pour in the mixture, and refrigerate until set. Turn onto a serving plate and fill the center with whipped cream.

Lemon Scented Baked Custard

3 eggs
2 cups milk
2 tablespoons honey
A little margarine or butter
1 medium lemon scented geranium leaf

Preheat oven to 350°F

Break the eggs into an 8-inch square glass baking dish, add the honey, and gradually pour in the milk, beating with a fork. Dot with butter and place the geranium leaf on top. Place inside a larger cake pan with 2 inches of water in it, and bake at 350°F for 45 minutes. You may use a geranium leaf this way with rice pudding as well.

Steamed Date Pudding

3 tablespoons honey
4 tablespoons soft butter
½ pound pitted dates
5 tablespoons self-rising flour
⅓ cup soft bread crumbs
Pinch of salt
¼ teaspoon ground ginger
¼ teaspoon ground cinnamon
1 tablespoon sherry
2 tablespoons milk
1 egg

Cream the butter with the honey in a bowl. Chop the dates into fairly small pieces. Mix the flour, bread crumbs, salt, and spices together in a bowl; then blend into the butter and honey mix. Beat the sherry and milk with the egg in a bowl and add to the first mixture. Pour the mixture into a greased 4-cup (2 pint) pudding dish. Cover with tin foil and steam inside of a large covered pot with water for 2½ hours. Serve with golden syrup, custard or cream.

Date and Orange Flan

½ pound pitted dates
4 tablespoons stout (or any dark beer)
¼ teaspoon ground cardamom
¼ teaspoon ground cinnamon
2 oranges
1 precooked pie shell (page 44)

Precook one pie shell first. Chop and cook the dates in a saucepan over medium heat for 7–10 minutes with the stout and spices until the mixture is like thick jam.

Grate the rind of one of the oranges, and peel the other one. Discard the peel, and slice the oranges into thin, crosswise slices. Snip out the inner white pits with scissors; remove all pits. Spread the date mixture in the bottom of the precooked pastry shell and arrange the orange slices in a circle round the top, sprinkle with the grated rind, pour golden syrup on top, and leave to set.

Dutch Biscuits

1¼ cup self-rising flour
Pinch of salt
½ teaspoon mixed spice
1 teaspoon cinnamon
1–2 tablespoons margarine
⅓ cup honey
Grated rind of ½ lemon
1⅓ cup almonds, ground
3 tablespoons shortbread cookie crumbs
Slivered almonds

Preheat oven to 350°F

Sift the flour, salt, and spices together in a bowl. Cream the margarine and honey together in a separate bowl; add the lemon rind, ground almonds, shortbread crumbs, and flour mixture. Mix well, then knead on a floured surface until smooth. Roll the dough out very thin, less than ¼-inch thickness, and cut into the shapes of your choice, or into 2½-inch circles (using the floured edge of a wine glass for your cutting tool!). Scatter the slivered almonds on top and press them lightly into the biscuits. Bake on a greased cookie sheet at 350°F for 10–14 minutes. Lift off with a spatula and cool on a wire rack.

Fruit Cream

½ cup cottage cheese
1 tablespoon lemon juice
2 tablespoons honey
1 small eating apple
1 pear
5 cherries
½ orange
A few grapes
1 tablespoon grated nuts

Blend the cheese and lemon juice together in a bowl to a smooth, creamy consistency; then blend in the honey. Chop all the fruit into very small pieces, add to the cheese mix, and serve in glass dishes, sprinkled with nuts. Serves four.

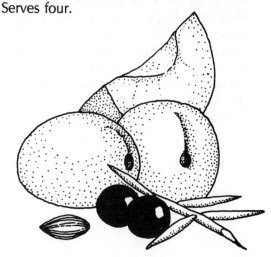

Fruit Salad with Pecan Dressing

2 red apples
2 pears
3 ripe bananas, sliced
1 cup canned pineapple, cubed
½ pound seedless grapes
1 teaspoon honey
¼ cup shelled pecans
1 cup whipping cream
½ cup orange juice
1 tablespoon lemon juice

Peel the pears, but not the apples; then core and dice them both and place in a large serving bowl. Add the sliced bananas, cubed pineapple, grapes, and honey. Bake the pecans on a cookie sheet at 350°F for 10 minutes to enhance their flavor, then chop. Whip the whipping cream, blend in the orange and lemon juices, fold in the pecans, and finally fold into the fruit mixture. Serves eight.

Fresh Fruit Salad with Cranberry Dressing

2–3 ripe peaches
3 ripe bananas
1 large fresh pineapple or
    1 large (17-ounce) can sliced pineapple
4 tablespoons mayonnaise
½ cup cranberry jelly sauce
Juice of ½ lemon
Juice of ½ orange
2 teaspoons honey

Cut all the fruit into bite-sized pieces, and mix together in a serving bowl. In a separate bowl, blend together the mayonnaise, cranberry sauce, lemon and orange juices, and honey. Serve the fruit salad, with the dressing on the side. Serves from six to eight.

Fruit Trifle

1½ cups corn flakes
3½ tablespoons milk
1½ tablespoons honey
2 medium eating apples
2 bananas, mashed
1 cup whipping cream
A few purple or green grapes

Crush the corn flakes in a bowl, mix with 1½ tablespoons of milk and honey, and place in the bottom of an 8-inch square baking dish. Grate the apples into a bowl, add the mashed bananas, and 2 tablespoons of milk; mix well and spread on top of the corn flakes. Whip the whipping cream and spread a thick layer on top of the fruit. Decorate with the de-seeded grapes.

Chill for 2 hours in the refrigerator.

Ginger Biscuits

2 cups flour
5 tablespoons ground ginger
18 tablespoons (½ pound) margarine
⅓ cup honey

Preheat oven to 375°F

Sift the flour and ginger together in a bowl, cut in the butter with a pastry cutter, and stir in the honey. Knead on a floured surface until smooth; then roll out very thin, and cut into 2½-inch circles. Arrange on a greased cookie sheet and bake at 375°F for 25–30 minutes.

Ginger Sponge Pudding

6 tablespoons margarine or butter
2½ tablespoons honey
1 egg
1½ tablespoons golden or corn syrup
¾ cup self-rising flour
2 teaspoons ground ginger
1 teaspoon mixed spice
Pinch of salt
Warm syrup as sauce

Cream the butter and honey together in a bowl until well-blended, then beat in the egg and syrup. Using a flour sifter, sift the flour, ginger, mixed spice, and salt into the butter mixture; stir well. Pour the mixture into a greased 4 cup (2 pint) pudding dish, cover tightly with tin foil, and steam inside a large covered pot with water for 1¾ hours. Be sure to check the water level from time to time; don't let the steam pot run dry! Serve with warmed syrup (diluted with a little lemon juice if you like) over the pudding.

Suppertime Ginger Pudding

2½ cups flour
1½ teaspoons baking powder
1 teaspoon baking soda
½ teaspoon salt
1½ teaspoons cinnamon
1½ teaspoons ground ginger
¼ teaspoon nutmeg
½ cup seedless raisins
½ cup walnuts, chopped
2 tablespoons dark molasses
¾ cup honey
2 eggs
2 tablespoons margarine

Preheat oven to 350°F

Sift all the dry ingredients together in a bowl. Mix a cupful of this with the raisins and nuts in a separate bowl. Cut the margarine into the dry ingredients, using a pastry cutter. Blend in 1 cup of boiling water, add the floured nuts and raisins, and stir well. Mix the honey, molasses, and eggs in a bowl, beat well, and blend into the first mixture. Pour into a greased cake pan and bake at 350°F for 50–60 minutes. Serve hot as a pudding, or cold as a cake.

Gingerbread Feather Cake

12 tablespoons margarine
¼ cup honey
2 eggs
¾ cup dark molasses
1¼ cups self-rising flour
½ teaspoon baking soda
¾ teaspoon ground ginger
1 teaspoon cinnamon
½ teaspoon nutmeg
6 tablespoons stout or milk
6 tablespoons water

Preheat oven to 350°F

Melt the margarine in a saucepan over low heat, then blend in the honey, eggs, and molasses. Sift all the dry ingredients together in a large bowl and beat into the first mixture. Heat the stout and water in a saucepan over high heat until very hot, then beat it into the mixture. Line a greased 11½ x 9-inch cake pan with wax paper. Brush the wax paper with melted margarine and pour in the mix. Bake at 350°F for 40–45 minutes. Do not turn out of the pan until cold, then put on a wire rack. Serve plain or with a butter icing.

Honey Biscuits

1¼ cups honey
8 tablespoons margarine
2½ cups whole wheat flour
1 teaspoon baking soda
4 tablespoons milk
2 teaspoons crushed coriander seeds

Preheat oven to 400°F

Heat the honey and margarine in a saucepan over medium-high heat until it bubbles, then pour into a bowl. Sift in the flour and baking soda, add the milk and crushed coriander seeds; stir well and chill. Roll out on a floured surface to 1-inch thickness, cut into biscuit-shapes, and bake on a greased and floured baking pan with shallow sides at 400°F for 15 minutes. Leave on the pans until cold; store in closed cans.

Orange Delish

4 large oranges
4 egg whites
4 tablespoons marmalade
3 tablespoons honey
Whipped cream

Cut the oranges in half; scoop out and discard the insides, leaving just the shells. Beat the egg whites in a bowl with an egg beater until stiff but not dry. Beat in the marmalade and honey with a wooden spoon. Grease the top and sides of a double boiler, pour in the mixture, and cover. Cook over medium-high heat for 50 minutes over hot water without removing the cover. Turn out and fill the orange halves, cool, and serve with whipped cream. Looks very pretty decorated with canned orange or mandarin slices.

Peach or Mango Mousse

½ teaspoon agar-agar powder or
  1 stick agar-agar
4 tablespoons warm water
½ cup honey
1 teaspoon ground ginger
1 cup water or
  ½ cup each fruit syrup and water
2 large ripe mangoes or peaches, fresh or
  1 large (17-ounce) can
2 eggs, separated
1 cup whipping cream, whipped stiff
Garnish of shredded coconut, toasted

Dissolve the agar-agar in a bowl with 4 table-spoons of warm water. Simmer the honey and ginger together in a saucepan with 1 cup of water over low heat for a few minutes. If you are using canned fruit, use ½ cup of the syrup and ½ cup of water, instead of just 1 cup of water. Peel, slice, and simmer the raw fruit in the syrup-honey water over low heat until tender; then blend in the blender. Add the dissolved agar-agar and beat in the egg yolks. Stir over very low heat until smooth and thickened, but do not boil; remove from the heat, and cool slightly. Whip the whipping cream and egg whites separately to the stiff peak stage, and fold gently into the mixture. Pour into a bowl or individual dishes and chill in the refrigerator. Just before serving, sprinkle the tops with toasted, shredded coconut which gives a delightful crispness in contrast to the bland mousse.

Baked Pears and Cardamom

4–5 pears
1 tablespoon honey
1 tablespoon wine or water
1 teaspoon cardamom seeds, cracked
Cream

Preheat oven to 350°F

Peel, core, and slice the pears into a shallow baking dish, add the honey and wine, and sprinkle with the cracked cardamom seeds (crack them with a rolling pin). Bake at 350°F until the pears are soft (approximately 30–45 minutes). Leave to cool. Serve this delicately flavored dish with a little cream.

Glazed Pears

4 large ripe pears
Butter or margarine
1 teaspoon cinnamon or
   4 crushed coriander seeds
Honey for fillings
½ cup honey
1 cup water
1 cup passion fruit pulp, puréed or
   1 cup black currant purée
A few pieces of angelica herb
Cream

Wipe and core the pears from the stem end. Place inside the cored section of each one: a dab of butter, 1 crushed coriander seed or ¼ teaspoon cinnamon, and a few drops of honey. Boil the ½ cup of honey with 1 cup of water together in a saucepan over high heat for 10 minutes. Add the pears, spoon the syrup over them, cover the pan, and simmer gently over low heat until just tender (spooning the syrup over them frequently). Lift the pears out very carefully onto a serving dish. Stir the chosen purée into the syrup, pour the syrup over the pears, and place an angelica stalk into each pear. Chill and serve with cream.

Poppy Seed Cake

1½ cups poppy seeds, ground
6 eggs, separated
¾ cup honey
1 teaspoon allspice
Pinch of salt
½ cup mixed peel, cut
Whipped cream

Preheat oven to 325°F

Grind the poppy seeds in a blender if you cannot buy them already ground. Beat the egg yolks until well-blended; then, still beating, dribble in the honey, stir in the spice, poppy seed, salt, and peel. Pour the mixture into a greased spring form pan and bake at 325°F for 50 minutes. Leave the cake in the pan until cool, then remove the spring form. Spread the cake with whipped cream and serve at once.

Pound Cake

1 cup (½ pound) margarine
½ cup honey
4 eggs
1⅔ cup flour
Grated rind of 1 lemon
4 tablespoons lemon or orange peel,
　finely chopped
1 cup currants
1 cup raisins

Preheat oven to 300°F

Cream the margarine and honey together in a bowl. Beat the eggs and add, alternately with the flour, to the margarine. Mix well, then add the rest of the ingredients. Pour into a greased and floured cake pan and bake at 300°F for 2 hours.

Prune Whip

1 pound prunes, cooked and pitted
3 egg whites
2 tablespoons lemon juice
⅓ cup honey
1 teaspoon grated lemon rind
Pinch of salt

Cook 1 pound of prunes in a saucepan with 2 cups of water over medium heat until softened. Drain and pit. Put all the ingredients in a deep bowl and beat with an electric beater until the mixture is well-blended. Chill and serve with cream.

Rhubarb with Angelica Leaves

4–5 stalks rhubarb
1 cup water
⅓ cup honey
2 thin curls of lemon peel
4 young angelica leaves
Yogurt

Wipe and cut the rhubarb into 1-inch pieces; simmer until tender in a saucepan over low heat with 1 cup of water, honey, lemon peel, and angelica leaves. Serve with yogurt.

Rhubarb Slices

3 tablespoons whipping cream
¾ pound (3 large stalks) rhubarb
⅓ cup honey
¼ cup water
2 tablespoons butter or margarine
4 slices whole wheat bread

Whip the whipping cream with an electric beater or egg beater until stiff; chill. Wipe and cut the rhubarb into 1-inch pieces; simmer with the honey and ¼ cup of water in a saucepan over low heat for 10–15 minutes, until the fruit is soft but not falling apart. Melt the butter in a frying pan over medium heat and fry the bread slices until golden brown on both sides. Serve the rhubarb over the bread with whipped cream. Serve hot or cold.

Rebanades

4 thick slices of bread
1 egg
½ teaspoon salt
½ cup milk
Olive oil
Honey
Cinnamon

Remove the crusts and cut the bread into triangles. Beat the egg and salt into the milk in a bowl, then soak the bread in this mixture for 1 minute. Heat ½ inch of olive oil in a frying pan until very hot, but not smoking (350°F). Deep-fry the triangles in the oil until golden on both sides. Drain and serve spread with honey and sprinkled with cinnamon.

Russian Cream

¾ cup (6 ounces) cream cheese
1 cup milk
1 teaspoon lemon juice
2½ tablespoons honey
½ cup raisins, mixed
½ cup nuts, grated

Blend the cheese and milk together in a bowl to a thick, creamy consistency. Add the remaining ingredients, mix well, and serve.

Saffron Buns

Saffron now comes from different parts of the world and is almost as precious as gold dust. When you want to use saffron threads, crush the required number and soak them in the hot liquid listed in the recipe. Prepare powdered saffron the same way, or sift it into the flour.

1 cup Half and Half or milk
16 tablespoons margarine (½ pound)
½ cup honey
2 large pinches saffron powder
3 eggs and 1 extra yolk
Salt
3 tablespoons dried yeast
1 teaspoon crushed coriander seeds
8¾ cups flour

Preheat oven to 400°F

Heat the milk, margarine, and honey together in a saucepan over medium-low heat until warm and blended; add the saffron and remove from the heat to let cool to lukewarm. Mix the eggs and extra yolk with the salt, yeast, and coriander seeds in a bowl. Sift the flour into a separate large bowl and add the rest of the ingredients to it. Mix and then knead. Make into small cakes or buns, let them rise until doubled in bulk, and then bake at 400°F until done.

Saffron and Gooseberry Shortcake

1⅓ cups self-rising flour
¼ teaspoon powdered saffron
¼ teaspoon salt
¼ cup honey
8 tablespoons butter
1 egg
½ cup milk
1 pound, or 1 large (17-ounce) can, gooseberries
2 teaspoons arrowroot, blended with a little milk
Cream

Preheat oven to 400°F

Sift the flour, saffron and salt into a bowl, add the honey, cut in the fat and add the egg and milk. Put in a greased 8-inch pan and bake at 400°F for 15 minutes. Cool slightly and turn out onto a wire rack. Stew the gooseberries or better still, use a large (17-ounce) can of gooseberries. Pour the liquid into a pan and simmer to reduce it a little, then thicken it with the arrowroot mixed with a little milk. When thickened, pour over the cake and serve with cream.

Simnel Cake

1 cup butter or margarine
½ cup honey
3 large eggs
1⅔ cups self-rising flour
½ teaspoon grated nutmeg
½ teaspoon mixed spice
2 cups currants
¾ cup raisins
1½ cups golden raisins
5 tablespoons cut mixed peel
4 tablespoons glacé cherries, halved
1 pound almond paste
Apricot jam

Preheat oven to 350°F

Cream the butter and honey together in a bowl, then beat in the eggs, one at a time. Sift the flour and spices together, add to the creamed mixture, then mix in the fruit. Grease and line with wax paper a round 8-inch cake pan and pour in half the cake mixture. Spread ¾'s of the almond paste on top of the cake mixture, then pour on the rest of the cake mixture. Bake at 350°F for 45 minutes, lower the heat to 320°F, and bake for 2 more hours. Do not turn out of the pan until the cake is cold. Turn it upside down, place a neat small circle of almond paste in the center, and spread with warmed apricot jam around the almond circle. Roll the rest of the paste into twelve small balls and place around the top circle. Brown the top lightly under the broiler.

Seed Sponge Cake

3 eggs, separated
⅓ cup honey
⅔ cup self-rising flour
Pinch of salt
1½ tablespoons arrowroot or cornstarch
2 tablespoons water
2 teaspoons margarine, softened
1 tablespoon orange flower water or water
1 tablespoon caraway seed

Preheat oven to 400°F

Beat the egg whites until stiff and dry, then gently stir in the honey and egg yolks. Sift the flour, salt, and arrowroot together several times in a bowl, and fold lightly into the egg mixture. Heat the water, margarine and orange flower water in a saucepan over low heat for 10 minutes until blended and warm. Fold into the egg mixture with the caraway seeds. Pour into a greased and floured cake pan and bake at 400°F for 20 minutes.

Spanish Cream

¾ teaspoon agar-agar powder or
⅔ stick agar-agar
⅓ cup honey
Pinch of salt
2½ cups milk
½ teaspoon almond extract
3 eggs, separated

Mix the agar-agar, honey, salt, and milk in the top of a double boiler; let stand for 5 minutes. Cook and stir over simmering water until the agar-agar is dissolved. Beat the egg yolks slightly, stir into the hot milk, and cook until the custard will coat the back of a spoon (about 15 minutes). Cool for 10 minutes and add the extract. Beat the egg whites until glossy with folding peaks. Pour the custard into a bowl, fold in the egg whites, pour into custard cups or small molds, and chill. Serve very cold.

Sesame and Oatmeal Cookies

8 tablespoons (1 cube) butter or
margarine, melted
¼ cup honey
1⅓ cups rolled oats
¼ cup sesame seeds
1 level teaspoon salt
¾ cup desiccated coconut

Preheat oven to 375°F

Melt the butter with the honey in a saucepan over low heat. Mix all the dry ingredients together in a bowl, add the melted butter and honey, and mix well. Press into a greased and floured 8 x 8-inch cake pan. Bake at 375°F for ½ hour. Leave in the pan to cool, then cut into finger-sized slices.

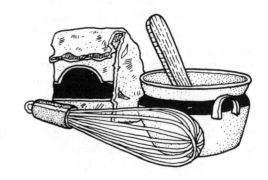

Spiced Tea Cake

1 apple
1 tablespoon butter
¼ cup honey
1 egg
⅔ cup self-rising flour
Pinch of salt
1 cup milk
Honey
1 teaspoon nutmeg
2 teaspoons crushed coriander seeds

Preheat oven to 350°F

Peel, core, and thinly slice the apple. Cream the butter and honey together in a bowl, add the egg, and beat well. Sift the flour with a pinch of salt and add it alternately with the milk to the butter mixture. Grease and flour a cake pan, arrange the sliced apple on the bottom, dot with honey, and sprinkle on nutmeg and coriander seeds. Pour the cake batter on top and bake at 350°F for 30 minutes. Lift carefully out of the pan and put on a plate or wire rack. May be eaten hot or cold.

Tapioca Lá Place

3 cups milk
1 vanilla pod
⅓ cup quick cooking tapioca or sage
2½ tablespoons honey
1 egg yolk
⅓ cup whipping cream
4 glacé cherries

Heat the milk and vanilla pod in a saucepan over high heat until just boiling; slowly stir in the tapioca, reduce the heat to low, and cook until the tapioca is transparent (15–20 minutes). Remove from the heat, lift out the vanilla pod, and whisk in the honey and egg yolk. Leave to cool, stirring often to prevent a "skin" from forming on the top. Pour into 4 glasses or dishes and chill. Whip the whipping cream to the stiff peak stage, pile on top of each serving, and decorate with a cherry.

Walnut Macaroons

4 egg whites
¼ teaspoon salt
½ cup honey
3 cups crushed corn flakes
1 cup coconut
1 teaspoon almond extract
1 cup walnuts, coarsely chopped

Preheat oven to 350°F

Beat the egg whites and salt in a bowl to a foamy, but not stiff texture. Add the honey a little at a time, and beat into a smooth, glossy mixture. Fold in, in the order given: the corn flakes, coconut, almond extract, and nuts. Drop from a teaspoon onto a well-greased cookie sheet. Bake at 350°F for about 15 minutes. Remove at once from the cookie sheet and cool on a wire rack.

Velvet Chiffon Cake

1½ cups flour
1¾ teaspoons baking powder
1 level teaspoon salt
¾ cup honey
¼ cup salad oil
Juice from 2 oranges mixed with water
   to make ⅔ cup
2 tablespoons grated orange peel
5 eggs, separated
3 tablespoons honey
¾ teaspoon cream of tartar

Preheat oven to 300°F

Sift together the flour, baking powder, and salt in a bowl. Blend in the honey, salad oil, orange juice, grated orange peel, and egg yolks; beat until smooth. Whisk the egg whites with the cream of tartar until they are stiff but not dry, then gradually add 3 table-spoons of honey to the egg whites and beat to a very stiff meringue. Gently fold the egg yolk mixture into the egg whites, making sure that it is perfectly blended. Turn into an ungreased cake pan, and bake at 300°F for 65–70 minutes. Invert the pan when the cake is cooked but do not try to take it out. It will drop out when it is ready.

Yorkshire Treacle Tart

PASTRY:
1¼ cups whole wheat flour
1 teaspoon baking powder
Pinch of salt
6–8 tablespoons butter or margarine
¾ cup cold water

FILLING:
3 tablespoons golden or corn syrup
2 teaspoons lemon juice
1 teaspoon grated lemon rind
3 heaping tablespoons soft bread crumbs
1 teaspoon cinnamon

Preheat oven to 350°F

Sift the flour, baking powder, and salt together in a bowl; cut in the butter with a pastry cutter or knife; and stir well, adding enough cold water to make a firm dough. Roll out on a floured surface. Line a pie plate with the pastry, trim and fold in the edges, and pinch up a rim. Prick with a fork or skewer on the bottom of the pie.

Using a hot measuring spoon, measure the golden syrup into a saucepan, add the lemon juice, rind, and bread crumbs, and warm slightly over low heat, stirring until well-mixed. Pour into the pastry lining and sprinkle with cinnamon. Bake at 350°F for 25-30 minutes. Serve cold or warm, not hot.

Zabaglione

4 egg yolks
5 teaspoons honey
½ cup Marsala wine or Madeira

Beat the egg yolks and honey together in a bowl until they are a pale primrose color. Add the Marsala and blend. Cook over boiling water in the top of a double boiler, beating all the time, but make sure the mixture does not boil. When it begins to rise in the pan, take off the heat and serve in glasses. Serve hot or cold.

Appendix

Measure Conversions

Dash . . . . less than ⅛ teaspoon
3 teaspoons . . . . 1 tablespoon (½ fluid ounce)
2 tablespoons . . . . ⅛ cup (1 fluid ounce)
4 tablespoons . . . . ¼ cup (2 fluid ounces)
5⅓ tablespoons . . . . ⅓ cup (2⅔ fluid ounces)
8 tablespoons . . . . ½ cup (4 fluid ounces)
10⅔ tablespoons . . . . ⅔ cup (5⅓ fluid ounces)
12 tablespoons . . . . ¾ cup (6 fluid ounces)
14 tablespoons . . . . ⅞ cup (7 fluid ounces)
16 tablespoons . . . . 1 cup
1 gill . . . . ½ cup
1 cup . . . . 8 fluid ounces
2 cups . . . . 1 pint
2 pints . . . . 1 quart (approx. 1 liter)
4 quarts . . . . 1 gallon
8 quarts . . . . 1 peck
4 pecks . . . . 1 bushel
1 gram . . . . 0.035 ounces
1 ounce . . . . 28.35 grams
16 ounces . . . . 1 pound (453.59 grams)
1 kilogram . . . . 2.21 pounds

Equivalent Temperatures: Celsius and Farenheit

°C	= °F		°C	= °F
150	302		45	113
145	293		40	104
140	284		35	95
135	275		30	86
130	266		25	77
125	257		20	68
120	248		15	59
115	239		10	50
110	230		5	41
105	221		0	32
100	212		-5	23
95	203		-10	14
90	194		-15	5
85	185		-20	-4
80	176		-25	-13
75	167		-30	-22
70	158		-35	-31
65	149		-40	-40
60	140			
55	131			
50	122			

Metric Conversion

To Change	To	Multiply By
ounces (oz.)	grams (g)	28
pounds (lbs.)	kilograms (kg)	0.45
teaspoons (tsp.)	milliliters (ml)	5
tablespoons (tbl.)	milliliters (ml)	15
fluid ounces (oz.)	milliliters (ml)	30
cups (c.)	liters (l)	0.24
pints (pt.)	liters (l)	0.47
quarts (qt.)	liters (l)	0.95
gallons (gal.)	liters (l)	3.8

Celsius and Farenheit

To convert Fahrenheit into Celsius (Centigrade), subtract 32, multiply by 5, divide by 9. $°F - 32 \times 5 \div 9 = °C$

To convert Celsius into Fahrenheit, reverse the formula: multiply by 9, divide by 5, add 32. $°C \times 9 \div 5 + 32 = °F$

Buying Calendar for Fresh Fruits and Vegetables

MONTH	FRUITS		VEGETABLES	
January	Apples Avocados Grapefruit Lemons	Navel oranges Tangerines Winter pears	Beets Cabbage Cauliflower Celery	Lettuce Potatoes Spinach
February	Apples Avocados Grapefruit Lemons	Navel oranges Tangerines Winter pears	Artichokes Beets Broccoli Cabbage Cauliflower	Celery Lettuce Potatoes Spinach
March	Apples Avocados Grapefruit	Lemons Navel oranges Winter pears	Artichokes Asparagus Beets Broccoli Cabbage	Carrots Cauliflower Celery Potatoes Spinach
April	Apples Avocados Grapefruit Lemons	Navel oranges Strawberries Winter pears	Artichokes Asparagus Beets Broccoli Carrots	Cauliflower Lettuce Peas Spinach
May	Avocados Cherries Grapefruit Lemons	Navel oranges Valencia oranges Strawberries	Asparagus Beets Cabbage Carrots Celery Lettuce	Onions Peas Potatoes Spinach Sweet corn Tomatoes
June	Apricots Avocados Bushberries Cantaloupe Cherries Figs Honeydew melon	Lemons Nectarines Peaches Plums Strawberries Valencia oranges Watermelon	Carrots Celery Cucumbers Green (snap) beans Lettuce Tomatoes	Onions Peppers Potatoes Summer squash Sweet corn
July	Apricots Avocados Bushberries Cantaloupe Grapefruit Honeydew melon Lemons	Nectarines Peaches Pears Plums Strawberries Valencia oranges Watermelon	Cabbage Carrots Celery Cucumbers Eggplant Green (snap) beans Green lima beans Tomatoes	Lettuce Okra Onions Peppers Potatoes Summer squash Sweet corn

Buying Calendar for Fresh Fruits and Vegetables

MONTH	FRUITS		VEGETABLES	
August	Avocados Cantaloupe Figs Grapes Grapefruit Honeydew melon Lemons	Nectarines Peaches Pears Persian melon Valencia oranges Watermelon	Cabbage Celery Cucumbers Eggplant Green (snap) beans Green lima beans Lettuce	Okra Onions Peppers Potatoes Summer squash Sweet corn Tomatoes
September	Apples Cantaloupe Figs Grapes Grapefruit Honeydew melon	Lemons Peaches Pears Persian melon Plums and prunes Valencia oranges	Cabbage Cucumbers Eggplant Green (snap) beans Green lima beans Lettuce	Onions Peas Peppers Summer squash Sweet corn Tomatoes
October	Apples Dates Figs Grapes Lemons	Pears Persian melon Persimmons Valencia oranges	Broccoli Brussels sprouts Cabbage Carrots Cucumbers Eggplant Green (snap) beans Green lima beans Lettuce	Okra Peas Peppers Potatoes Sweet corn Sweet potatoes Tomatoes Winter squash
November	Almonds Apples Avocados Dates	Grapes Lemons Persimmons Walnuts	Broccoli Brussels sprouts Cabbage Carrots Cauliflower Celery Eggplant Green (snap) beans	Lettuce Peas Peppers Potatoes Sweet corn Sweet potatoes Winter squash
December	Almonds Apples Avocados Dates	Grapefruit Lemons Navel oranges Walnuts	Broccoli Brussels sprouts Carrots Cauliflower	Celery Spinach Sweet potatoes Winter squash

Index